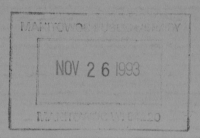

# DRIVING

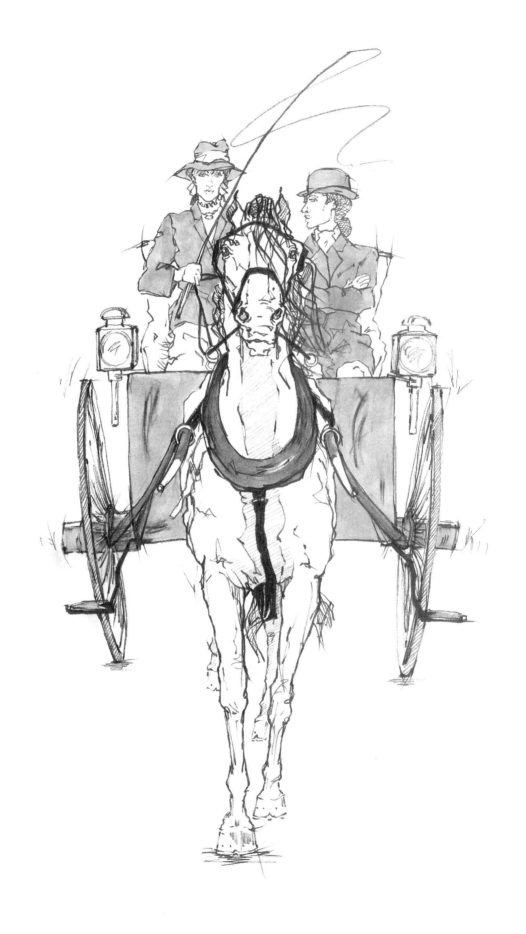

# DRIVING

## An Instructional Guide to Driving Singles and Pairs

## Clive Richardson

B.T. Batsford Ltd · London

First published 1993

© Clive Richardson 1993

Typeset by Servis Filmsetting Ltd,
Manchester
and printed in Great Britain by
Butler and Tanner, Frome, Somerset

Published by
B.T. Batsford Ltd
4 Fitzhardinge Street
London W1H 0AH

A catalogue record for this book is available
from the British Library

ISBN 0 7134 6946 3

# CONTENTS

# ACKNOWLEDGEMENTS

The author and publishers would like to thank the following:

For the line drawings: Jennifer Buxton, Sue Millard and Carole Vincer; and for the decorative artwork: Gabrielle Ceriden Morse.

For the photographs: Barrow Evening Mail (3), Charles Donaldson (13), Ken Ettridge (1, 5, 14, 17, 18, 21, 23, 26, 29, 35, 48), P. Higby (7), S. Millard (20, 22, 25), Stuart Newsham (2, 40, 41), R. Nienstedt (47), Phaneuf-Gurdziel (19), A. Reynolds (11), and Fred Wilson (43), Exmoor Pony Society (6), Tracey Elliot-Reep (27).

Special thanks also to Bill Jones, New York; Mary Nygaard, Florida; Gordon T. Heard, Virginia; Carolyn Sharp, Colorado; The Haflinger Association of America; Wendy Glenister; The Exmoor Pony Society; Diana Staveley; Roger M. Bass, The Highland Pony Society; Valerie Russell; Elizabeth Newboult-Young; Anne McCaig, The Dales Pony Society; Barbara Stoddart; and Sylvia Sullivan, my copy editor, for her help and support.

# FOREWORD

Upwards of eighty years ago, the ability to drive a horse in harness with reasonable competence was considered as much an everyday necessity as a social skill, and the majority of the adult population of Victorian and Edwardian times were as capable with driving reins and a whip as modern road users are behind the wheel of a motorcar.

Then, within the short space of one generation, all those skills learned and developed over centuries of driving horses were nearly lost as progress gave us faster and more convenient means of transport and the horse and carriage became outdated and obsolete as a result.

While horse-drawn travel and the use of horsepower in commerce and industry are now a thing of the past, driving for pleasure is very much a modern pursuit on both sides of the Atlantic with a growing number of enthusiasts keen to learn the traditions and skills of this ageless sport.

This book, which comprehensively covers all aspects of driving from the choice of a suitable horse, vehicle and harness to breaking and training, driving technique, vehicle restoration and competitive work should be a welcome addition to the library of literature now available on the subject and should provide a basic introductory guide for beginners as well as a reference book for future use.

George Bowman

1   Mr Garth Maddocks driving his Welsh cob, Taffy, to a ralli car

# PREFACE

Carriage driving is one of the fastest growing equestrian sports. Since being rediscovered in the 1950s as a leisure activity, it has attracted a large following of enthusiasts keen to learn the art of driving and the traditions of what is indisputably the oldest of all equestion disciplines.

Few, if any, of the people who witnessed the demise of the horse in favour of steampower and the internal combustion engine earlier this century could have expected driving to have made the comeback it has. Seeing no future for the horse and carriage, they were responsible for thousands of vehicles being broken up or left to rot in fields, harness being burned, and stables turned into garages. Ironically, a few decades later, these same people who had driven horses as a way of life were being called upon to advise and instruct a new generation of whips who were to revive and develop the sport and ensure that many of the old crafts like wheelwrighting and harness-making, which might have been lost, came back into demand.

The appeal of driving is not specific. For some people it affords the opportunity to take up an equestrian sport where two or more people can be actively involved at one time using the same horse. Whether driving competitively or merely for plea-sure, it can involve all members of a family as well as non-riders or even non-horsey friends who invariably enjoy the novelty and experience of being taken out for a drive.

For others, who may have ridden pre-viously, driving offers the challenge of a new and entirely different equestrian activity. Training a horse hitherto reserved only for riding to go in harness can increase the versatility, performance scope and value of the animal while bringing enhanced interest for the owner.

Many parents find driving gives them the opportunity to maintain an equestrian interest after their children have grown up, given up riding and left home, and sometimes an outgrown children's pony which might otherwise be pensioned off at grass is given a new purpose in life between shafts.

From a competitive point of view, driving encompasses a wide variety of opportunities to compete in shows and events from club to national level. For those who have not been involved with horses previously, it probably gives relati-vely inexperienced people the chance to progress to a reasonable competitive standard far quicker than other eques-trian sports would, and without the expense of highly-priced performance horses. There are also those people who, because of injury or disability, are unable to ride competitively but who still wish to compete seriously and for them driving is often the answer.

For less ambitious people, summer picnic drives and rallies provide plenty of organized activities in the company of others who also drive just for pleasure.

Irrespective of the reasons for taking up driving or the aspirations of those involved, the basic principles are the same and should result in a well-trained animal correctly and safely harnessed to a sound and roadworthy vehicle and driven competently and with confidence. Once that standard has been attained, the real pleasures of driving will be discovered in areas as diverse as the spit and polish of show classes, the thrill of timed marathons, or just the timeless elegance of a leisurely afternoon drive through country lanes.

In a time of great change, technological advancement and scientific achievement, it is perhaps surprising that the horse and carriage are still with us and that horse drawn days, instead of being a vestige of the past, will accompany us into the future.

2   Driving encompasses a wide variety of opportunities to compete in shows and events from club to national level

3   Mr Fred Todd driving his Fell/Thoroughbred cross
gelding, Tom Kydd, to a cee-spring dogcart. Note the
integral shafts allowing the vehicle body to be built
wider without altering the shaft width for the horse

# Part 1
# MAKING A START

# 1
# CHOOSING A DRIVING HORSE

## *Selection Criteria*

The selection of a suitable animal to drive is likely to be governed by a number of criteria, which need to be carefully considered before making any decisions or purchases.

### Type of work

Foremost of these considerations is the type of work the horse or pony will be used for. A quiet, reliable and somewhat dull cob type is unlikely to have much impact in the showring, whereas the sort of horse that might catch the judge's eye because of its presence and spectacular action may not be ideal for quiet Sunday afternoon drives in the countryside. These days, most driving horses are ridden as well as driven, so the animal's requirements as a saddle horse could be a consideration, especially if it is to be used by several people or a family, and there is no reason why a driving horse should not hunt, jump or take part in riding club and other equestrian activities.

### Local terrain

The type of local terrain where the animal will be driven could influence the choice, as a stronger, more substantial type of horse would be better suited to steep, hilly country than a small pony of slender build, and it should be remembered that driving on smooth roads is less demanding than driving on sandy lanes, dirt tracks or rough ground. The number or size of people the horse is expected to convey, together with the weight of the vehicle, must also be an important consideration, with a subsequent bearing on the size and strength of the animal selected. In the same way that a tall rider can look under-horsed on a pony, a tall driver can look equally out of proportion sitting behind a diminutive pony in a cart of miniature dimensions.

### Facilities

The premises and facilities available could also be a deciding factor, as only a hardy animal would be able to live outside all year round if access to a stable were not possible and, more so, if the field were in an exposed location. Some form of protection from the worst of the weather, even if only a field shelter, should still be provided.

### Experience

The experience of the *whip* or driver must also have a considerable influence on the basis that two novices never go together successfully. A knowledgable horseman with a young horse is fine, and so is a newcomer to driving with an experienced horse, which has been driven extensively and knows his job inside out; but to put a novice behind an inexperienced horse is to court disaster.

### Finance

Lastly, the finance available could impose its own limitations. A well-bred, fully-trained young horse is not likely to be cheap, especially if it has some competitive experience behind it, but perfectly adequate and workmanlike driving horses that fully meet requirements can usually be found at considerably less expense. Prioritizing these requirements in order of importance can facilitate decision-making.

## Make and Shape

Driving horses and ponies come in all shapes, sizes, breeds, types and colours and it is fatuous to generalize on what is or is not a correct driving type. Upwards of seventy years ago, virtually all horses of whatever kind were broken to drive as well as ride. Nevertheless, some types are better suited to harness work than others, although few animals, correctly trained, will not go between shafts.

Basically, a good driving horse should be well built with a deep body and a broad chest to allow plenty of room for the heart and lungs. Shallow, narrow-fronted animals lacking stamina should be avoided as the physical demands on a driving horse can be great even with quiet drives out from home. A well-sprung rib cage, strong loins and powerful quarters are very desirable, and the tail should be well set on and not too low. While depth of shoulder is important, it is permissible to have a straighter and more upright shoulder in a driving horse than would be preferable in a riding horse. This is because a straight shoulder predisposes the animal to be an uncomfortable and rather jarring ride but this fault passes unnoticed when the animal is in harness. However, if the horse is to be ridden as well as driven, which is probable, then a well laid-back shoulder is important. As a general rule, the slope of the shoulder should correspond to the slope of both the pastern and the wall of the hoof.

### Conformation

A good length of neck is a desirable quality in any horse and it should be well muscled and strong with a well defined curve to the top line and no tendency to thickness in the gullet. A horse with a short, thick neck will always look stuffy in front, and a full collar on such an animal will simply emphasise the fault. Often it is difficult to find a collar to fit such a horse as they tend to sit awkwardly on the shoulders, and bull-necked horses frequently prove to be strong and liable to pull when driven as there is little flexion at the poll. Long, weak necks look equally bad, especially if they show a concave dip between the poll and withers although, if this is because of poor condition or immaturity rather than conformation, an improvement can usually be effected by means of correct feeding, muscling up exercises and regular work.

A good head is again of lesser importance in a driving horse than a riding horse as the blinkers mask to a degree a plain or even coarse head. A bold eye usually denotes a kind and generous nature.

The limbs are of vital importance in a driving horse as he is likely to do more of his work on the hard road than a riding horse even though he is not carrying any

**4** Cobs are among the most popular of all driving types of horse or pony

weight directly on his back. Even so, the concussion of shod hoofs on the unyielding road surface is likely to identify any weaknesses which may be there sooner or later, and horses that are short of bone or have poor-quality, round bone are best avoided. Instead, the ideal is short cannon bones with plenty of flat, flinty bone, clean joints, and dense, well-shaped hoofs. Large, flat, shelly feet, which are liable to break away around the edges, will present problems keeping shoes on, and small, upright, boxy feet are equally unsatisfactory, although some improvement can often be made by the work of a skilled farrier. Black or 'blue' hoofs are generally believed to be more resilient than white or striped hoofs.

A nicely-sloping pastern, another requisite of a good riding horse, is again of lesser importance in a harness horse, although it is worth remembering that the straighter the pastern, the less of a cushioning effect it has on the rest of the leg.

Hocks should be large and well defined. A tendency to go 'wide behind' is less objectionable than cow hocks as the former rarely affects the performance capabilities of the horse. Hauliers who used horses for draught work at the turn of the century often favoured horses which went 'wide behind' in the belief that it was a sign of strength.

Overall, a good harness horse should look balanced and symmetrical, with plenty of substance and a bold outlook.

## Action

The importance of action depends largely upon the type of work the animal will be used for but straight action, or as near to it as possible, is preferable. Faulty action, such as forging (when a horse strikes a fore-shoe with a hind usually at trot) or brushing (when one leg is struck with the opposite foot at the coronet or fetlock) can sometimes be rectified by remedial shoeing. Forging seldom causes injury, although the continual clicking noise can be irritating, and young horses or those in poor condition sometimes forge although maturity and condition respectively deal with the problem given time. Brushing can cause swelling, soreness or even lameness in which case protective boots are the only solution. Speedy cutting, which is similar to brushing except that the injury is inflicted higher up the leg, often on the inside of the knee, is less common but can be dealt with in the same way as brushing. Dishing (when one or both forefeet swing out sideways at the trot) and plaiting (when they do the opposite) are cosmetic faults in all but severe cases and rarely do more than detract from the animal's way of going.

Viewed from the side, a good horse will move freely from the shoulder, not just from the elbow, with a good length of stride which covers the ground, and with the hocks well engaged. Daisy-cutting action (which is low to the ground with the minimum amount of flexion of the knee) is untypical in a driving horse and can be dangerous when travelling on rough ground as it can cause the animal to stumble or even fall. More preferable is the type of 'round' action with a degree of bend to the knee and hock, although this must not be at the expense of reach. Individual breed societies will have an official breed standard, which sets out the requirements in terms of conformation, characteristics and action for their particular breed, and these should be referred to for additional information. With the exception of the Hackney, which is a specialised breed, excessive knee action is wasteful and unnecessary, and to sit

behind such an animal gives the impression of tremendous energy being expended with little actual progress being made. In the case of horses which are ridden as well as driven, excessively animated action is very uncomfortable and tiring for the rider and also increases the everyday wear and tear on the horse's legs.

Clearly-defined and active paces are essential. The walk should be free and balanced with a crisp four-time sequence of foot-falls, and the trot should be regular and even with no tendency to break pace or skip. A good horse will be able to absorb any increase in speed by lengthening his stride and maintaining the same rhythm rather than by quickening his pace. Pacing, which is where the horse moves both legs on the same side simultaneously instead of alternatively as in the trot, is incorrect except on the harness racing track and the proper gait is a two-time diagonal trot.

Some breeds, like the American Saddlebred, have specialized and distinctive additional paces including the slow rack or running walk and the fast rack in which the feet come down singly and with no pauses in a rapid four-time beat. As the name suggests, the Saddlebred is primarily a riding horse and, although many are driven, demonstrations of their extraordinary paces in harness are usually confined to specialist classes at their own shows. Icelandic ponies have also developed a running walk with the same four-beat sequence and known within the breed as the tolt.

## Temperament

The importance of the correct type of temperament in a driving horse cannot be over-stressed. A calm, sensible nature is worth a great deal. Horses with any inclination towards being flighty or nervous, or which are liable to hot up especially in company, or become fractious, are generally unsuitable for driving, particularly by a novice. If a horse shows any of these tendencies when ridden, they are unlikely to be overcome by putting it between shafts.

## Size

Size is of lesser importance, although very large or very small animals have their disadvantages. It is quite often difficult to find both harness and vehicles to fit animals at either end of the scale without going to the expense of made-to-measure harness and custom-built vehicles. Equipment for animals of intermediate size is more readily available and, consequently, more competitively priced. A big horse is more expensive to keep in terms of feeding and additional running costs like shoeing without there necessarily being any advantage for the owner. On the other hand, a small pony cannot be expected to undertake the same workload as a big horse, and his lack of inches precludes all but children from riding him if he is a dual-purpose ride and drive animal. In driving trials and some other competitive events, small ponies are at an immediate disadvantage as, even in pony classes, they are competing against larger animals on equal terms and a Shetland would be expected to maintain the same pace on a marathon as a 14.2 h.h. Connemara or New Forest. A pony-size turnout is, however, much easier to transport to shows, rallies or events, and can often be carried in a suitably modified double-pony trailer.

## Colour

Colour should be the least important of all the considerations governing the selection of a driving horse or pony. Only in the showring might the colour of the horse be of any real relevance as some more tra-

ditional judges can be prejudiced on the grounds that some colours are less appropriate than others in a showing class. Piebalds and skewbalds are most discriminated against by such judges, although personal preferences of this type should only have a bearing on the decision when the more important judging criteria have failed on balance to establish a clear placing order. Other judges can show a disdain for pale, wishy-washy colours or excessive white markings which they may feel are too flamboyant for a private driving class where a discreet and workmanlike appearance is required. People who aspire to driving a pair or tandem and who may be searching for another horse or pony to match the one already owned will find that some colours are easier to match than others. Bearing in mind the problems of finding two animals of similar size, type, action and stride, trying to match unusual colours can simply exacerbate the difficulties.

## *Breeds*

The wide range of horse and pony breeds and crosses suitable for driving offers tremendous variety and choice and, as most will fulfill the criteria already discussed, the final selection is likely to be dictated by personal preference.

### Shetland

Of the smaller breeds, the Shetland (5, 35) has long been popular as a driving pony as his diminutive size belies his great strength and stamina. A fit Shetland will easily pull a trap and two adults, and the breed's track record in combined driving events shows that they can make the kilometre speeds required for these demanding competitions. Although Shetlands may have short legs, good examples

5   Mr Tom Devine driving his Shetland pony to a country cart. Despite their diminutive size, Shetlands are immensely strong with great stamina and powers of endurance

of the breed move freely and have excellent ground-covering action and they can keep up with larger ponies on driving rallies.

## Caspian

The Caspian pony is another example of a pony breed which, despite its size, has both strength and endurance. Devotees of the breed, which is increasing in popularity, claim the Caspian is capable of remarkable feats of performance and, being narrower than the stockily-built Shetland, it is probably more suitable as a mount for young children if it is to be ridden as well as driven. However, it lacks the bone and substance of the Shetland and is not so

readily available, which has inevitably cost implications, whereas the ubiquitous Shetland enjoys world-wide distribution and is almost certainly the best known of all pony breeds.

Recently, Falabellas and other miniature breeds and types have been given a lot of publicity. However, their tiny size and general lack of substance make them unsuitable for serious driving, although they are shown in lightweight vehicles at their specialist shows.

## Dartmoor and Exmoor

Moving up the height range, the Dartmoor (27) and Exmoor (6) breeds are both noted for their toughness, hardiness and resilience. The Exmoor sometimes has a reputation for being intractable, but this is probably because ponies bred on the moors in a semi-feral state as the majority of Exmoors are take more time to come to

6 Mr and Mrs R.D. Wright's Exmoor pony, Knightcombe Dingy Footman, driven to a modern competition vehicle. Note the 'spares' basket strapped to the rear of the vehicle, and the umbrella basket under the mudguard

hand. Once handled and broken, they make good harness ponies and have the natural surefootedness of all true native breeds. The height limit for stallions is 12.3 h.h., with mares an inch smaller. The Dartmoor shares many of the Exmoor's qualities but is a prettier pony although not at the cost of stamina, and it stands up to 12.2 h.h. in height. As both Exmoors and Dartmoors breed very true to type, they are easier to match up for driving pairs than some other breeds, which may be a consideration for a long-term aim.

## Welsh ponies and cobs

Of all the pony breeds that are eminently suitable for driving, the Welsh ponies and cobs must be amongst the most popular. The Welsh Mountain or Section A (18, 34) is an exceptionally beautiful pony with great stamina and endurance, and many have achieved considerable success both in the showring and in performance events. The Welsh pony or Section B, which is larger and can stand up to 13.2 h.h., is essentially a riding pony and it tends to lack the native character and substance of its smaller ancestor. While the Section A displays the slight knee action that identifies it as a breed that has developed in rough or mountainous terrain, many Section Bs have acquired low, sweeping action, which makes them less suited to work between shafts. The Welsh pony of cob type or Section C is a much better driving type of animal and, although it does not exceed 13.2 h.h., it is an immensely strong and active pony with tireless energy and great character. Its larger counterpart, the Welsh Cob or Section D (1, 19, 40), is regarded by many to be one of the finest harness breeds in the world. It is a tremendously powerful animal combining all the best qualities of the Welsh Mountain pony (from which it is descended) with size and additional strength. The cob action is spectacular in good examples. The knee should flex but not excessively which would be wasteful, and the stride should be long and elastic and should cover the ground with ease. The hocks should flex well under the body, and the movement generally should appear robust, swift and animated.

## New Forest

The New Forest pony has been the subject of innumerable improvement programmes in the past, which have resulted in a considerable amount of alien blood being introduced. As a consequence, the New Forest pony has lost much of its consistency of type, with great variations in height, colour and stamp, although the breed has become more standardized in recent years. They make good driving ponies, being surefooted and quiet, and those which are reared on the forest are usually naturally impervious to traffic.

## Connemara

The Connemara, the only Irish pony breed, is another excellent all-rounder with good paces, a calm and generous nature, great intelligence, and hardiness of constitution. It excels as a ride and drive pony and takes an adult's weight.

## Highland

For people seeking a more substantial type of pony, the Highland (7, 28) combines immense strength with great docility but often at the cost of speed and agility of action. As with all the native breeds, hereditary unsoundness is unknown and they are long-lived and capable of living outside all year round.

## Fell and Dales

The Fell pony (12, 13, 16, 39, 43, 45), which stands up to 14 h.h., developed primarily as a pack pony and like the Dales (8, 29, 49), its larger cousin, makes an ideal harness breed as both are sturdy and powerful with good paces. In common with the Welsh Cob, Fells and Dales were used extensively for trotting races in the last century and a mile in three minutes at an extended trot was quite usual for these ponies. The popularity of combined driving in recent years has given Fell and Dales ponies an opportunity to demonstrate their performance capabilities, while others are used in riding and driving for the disabled projects where a placid nature is imperative.

## Norwegian Fjord

The Norwegian Fjord pony, outside of its country of origin, is generally more popular in America than in other parts of Europe. It is a distinctive cream-dun colour with a dark dorsal stripe, which runs from tail to forelock, and the mane is usually roached to make it stand up about 12 cm (5 ins) with the dark central part left a little higher than the cream-coloured sides. Its unusual and attractive colour tends to distract attention from its rather plain conformation, and its action is economical and a little lacking in length of stride. However, it is strong, hardworking and exceptionally kind.

8 Mrs M.G. Fitzgerald's Dales pony mare, Brymor Mimi, driven to a ralli car by Brian Marshall

## Haflinger

The Haflinger (9) developed as a light draught breed in the mountains of Austria where it was used extensively for agricultural work and in the forests. In recent years they have become popular for driving and their strength, surefootedness and inherent docility make them ideal for this type of work.

7 Mr David Rayner driving his Highland mares, Stromer of Alltnacailleach and Jeannie of Tenandry, in an obstacle cone driving competition. Penalty marks are incurred for hitting a cone and dislodging the ball from the top

## Native breed crosses

All of the native pony breeds make excellent foundation stock for cross-breeding although with such a diversity of type, size and colour within the pure breeds the purpose of crossing might be questioned. Sometimes the aim is to produce an animal of increased size and scope with more exuberant action by putting a stallion of one of the horse breeds onto a native pony mare. While the required qualities may be gained and without the loss of native stamina or constitution, the calm pony temperament that is so important in a driving horse may be sacrificed. A predominance of Thoroughbred, Hackney or Arab blood can predispose the animal to be highly-strung and volatile, although some excellent driving horses have been bred this way.

9 Mr and Mrs Delbert R. Rice's Haflinger stallion, Nitty Gritty, driven by Dr W.D. Smith at the American National Haflinger Show. The vehicle is a type of Meadowbrook

## Thoroughbred and Arab

Horse breeds offer as wide a variety as their pony counterparts. The Thoroughbred was developed as a riding horse and, more specifically, for racing. Its attributes, being based almost entirely on speed, are of little value in driving and, as the Thoroughbred temperament is not the most equable, few examples of the breed are seen in harness. A little Thoroughbred blood in a driving horse which is largely draught or pony bred can, nevertheless, add a degree of quality and elegance, and improve the overall action.

The Arab, from which the Thoroughbred is directly descended, is another breed really developed for riding, and purists may rightly point out that the breed hardly conforms to what is generally acknowledged to be driving type. Even so, in many parts of the world Arabs are driven and apart from their great beauty and elegance of movement they are possessed of exceptional stamina and endurance and are highly intelligent. As far as temperament is concerned, the Arab is more docile than the Thoroughbred, although many partbred Arabs (14, 46) are quite the opposite and Arab blood is less commonly sought in cross-bred driving horses than most other breeds.

## Hackney

Although the Hackney horse and Hackney pony (10, 31) evolved separately, one is merely a smaller version of the other and they share the same characteristics of ebullient high-stepping action and tremendous presence. Believed by many to be without equal as a harness animal, the Hackney's exuberant nature would almost certainly make it unsuitable for a novice to drive although there are the inevitable exceptions to disprove the rule. To meet showring standards the natural gait has been developed over many generations to an exaggerated shoulder, knee and hock action that makes them extremely uncomfortable to ride with the result that they are now essentially a harness breed.

## Continental Breeds

Continental breeds tend to come and go in fashion although a few have stood the test of time and become well established in the ranks of the driving fraternity. Some, like the Dutch Gelderlander or the German Oldenburg, are primarily harness breeds although their large size and stature make them more suited to coaching or team driving than single harness pleasure work. The English Cleveland Bay is similar. Others are of a more practical size and are more in line with the requirements of an amateur driver.

10 Mrs Wendy Skill driving her Hackney pony to a Liverpool gig in a private driving class. Many superb Liverpool gigs were built by the 19th century carriage builders, Lawton of London and Liverpool

## Friesian

The Friesian (33), which is of Dutch origin, is one of the oldest breeds in Europe and was a great favourite with funeral directors in the last century for drawing hearses because of its stately bearing, tractability and black colour. Other colours are unknown in the breed. Although many Friesians tend to be rather shallow in the body and narrow in front, they have considerable bone and substance and are generally willing and amenable workers. Their action shows elevation and poise making them surprisingly animated in movement for what is by definition a light draught breed.

## Lipizzaner

The Lipizzaner is often associated with the Spanish Riding School at Vienna but in addition to its qualities as a riding horse it is excellent in harness, being docile, intelligent and easy to train. Its colour, which is invariably grey, and its immense presence make it eye-catching and distinctive with consequent values in the showring.

## Morgan

America can boast several breeds that make good driving prospects and of these the Morgan (17, 21, 44) must take precedence. An all-round ride and drive animal, it should be compact, well built and muscular, with good paces and masses of stamina. Above all, the Morgan is a performance breed, and representatives have acquitted themselves with credit in virtually every equestrian discipline including driving since the breed was founded in the last century. Although the number of Morgan horses in Europe is limited, in their home country they are immensely popular for driving and deservedly so.

## Standardbred

Although the Standardbred was developed as a harness breed, its purpose was solely to race with speed as the ultimate goal, and other qualities were sacrificed to this end. In common with many of the harness racing horses in Europe, the breed incorporates pacers, which move laterally, as well as trotters, which move diagonally. The Standardbred is a big, well-made horse with the stamina to enable it to run heat after heat at race meetings without tiring, but it is inclined to lack quality or refinement, and many have very plain heads. In spite of the fact that it is bred to race, it is usually docile and the pleasure-driving market absorbs many rejects from the racetrack. However, as such rejects will only have ever been in a lightweight racing sulky, it is necessary to virtually break them in to drive from scratch to accustom them to the heavier equipment and different requirements of private driving. In addition, many have unresponsive or hard mouths as a result of race driving and need their mouths re-educating.

## Other types

As well as the more popular breeds, there are specific types of horse which are particularly well suited to harness work, most notably the cob. With the exception of the Welsh Cob, which is the only recognized breed of cob in the world, the term is generic and denotes a compact, deep-bodied and short-legged animal standing little more than about 15 h.h. and with an appearance that suggests endurance, power and activity. The action should be workmanlike, covering the ground with a good length of stride and with the slight knee and hock action desirable in a driving horse. The temperament is usually placid and kind. There is no guaranteed formula for the breeding of cobs but many trace their origins back to heavy cart mares or even heavyweight hunter types crossed with stallions of quality. A lot of the superb driving cobs bred in Ireland are a mixture of Irish Draught and Connemara pony with a splash of Thoroughbred or Hackney blood.

Although most of the pony breeds are ideal for driving, the show pony, which is really a type and not a breed even though it does have its own stud book, is, like many types developed for riding, not best suited to work between shafts. While it may possess great beauty and quality, it lacks the essential substance of a driving pony. Its low, daisy-cutting action is unsuited to driving purposes, and its legs are too fine to take a lot of regular road work. Many show ponies are rather volatile in nature, although some do adapt and disprove their reputation by years of service in harness.

## Draught breeds

While some people do drive representatives of the heavy draught breeds in single harness, their use is more usually confined to trade turnout classes at shows, or agricultural or commercial use. Clydesdales, Shires, Ardennes and all the other draught breeds were developed for the slow, heavy work at which they excel, and it is unreasonable to expect such an animal successfully to undertake the faster, lighter work usually associated with driving for pleasure. Also, being such large and impressive horses they tend to dwarf all but the more substantial trade vehicles, making the whole turnout appear imbalanced and out of proportion. However, some very fine driving horses with size, bone and showy action have been bred out of draught mares by Thor-

oughbred or, more particularly, Hackney stallions, and in most cases the docile nature of the draught horse has been inherited.

## Donkeys and mules

In briefly evaluating the driving qualities of some of the more popular breeds, it would be remiss not to mention the humble donkey (11). Despite an erroneous reputation for being stubborn and lazy, any problems of this sort can usually be traced back to inadequate basic training: as donkeys are generally very quiet, they are often assumed to know more than they do and their training may be hurried and sketchy. Ensuing problems are then blamed on the animal. Properly broken and schooled, donkeys can be very good in harness and many shows now include driven donkey classes in their schedules.

Mules and jennets have come back into popularity again in recent years. Their resilience and stamina is almost legendary and, depending on the breed of their parentage on the horse side, they can vary enormously in both type and size. Like donkeys, they need a comprehensive training programme but they make good driving animals, and their considerable performance potential makes them an interesting challenge.

## Buying a Driving Horse

For those who have not driven before or who have limited previous experience of horses generally, it is certainly advisable to buy a horse or pony that is already broken in and relatively experienced. A young and completely untrained animal is the least practical option usually, as the cost of having an animal professionally broken can soon swallow up any savings

11 Mrs Anne McCaig's pair of donkeys, Bonnie and Clyde, driven to a Malvern car. As well as competing very successfully in private driving classes, they regularly take part in all types of local driving club events

made by not buying an older, made and consequently more expensive horse. Breaking a horse yourself, assuming you have the background knowledge, requires skill as well as considerable time and patience plus access to a breaking vehicle of some description. Once broken in, a horse needs regular driving to give it experience before it can reasonably be called quiet to drive, and there is no guarantee that it will settle and be suitable for harness work. That aside, the satisfaction of having trained your own horse to drive is very rewarding.

## Where to look

When it comes to buying a driving horse, there are several ways of going about it. The best method is to buy an animal that you know and have seen driven regularly at rallies or shows or out on the roads. Your local driving club secretary or British Driving Society area commissioner (or, in America, an American Driving Society member) may be able to alert you to any likely animals coming on the market. A wanted advertisement in the club newsletter may also bring a response. If a horse or pony of a particular breed is required then the secretary or sales officer of the breed society may be able to help by putting you in touch with members who have stock to sell.

Answering advertisements in the equestrian press is slightly more risky as animals glowingly described in print frequently bear no resemblance in the flesh to your expectations, and much time and expense can be spent travelling around the country to see totally unsuitable animals. A photograph sent by the vendor can confirm what an animal looks like but offers little indication of its temperament or manners.

Horse sales have the advantage of gathering together in one place a selection of potentially suitable animals, although descriptions in the catalogue can be very misleading. Terms like 'driven in harness' really mean little at all and do not warrant the horse's fitness for driving, and more information can often be surmised not from what is said but from what is left unsaid. As horses are usually sold on their descriptions in the catalogue, this could have an implication on returning the animal, which many sales allow, if it turns out to have a fault not mentioned previously. Sometimes the catalogue will state that a particular animal can be seen and tried prior to sale day, which is an option worth taking up if the horse appears to match your requirements. In most cases, however, you may be bidding for an animal you have only seen driven on sale day, if at all, and many inexperienced purchasers have consequently learnt to their cost the foolishness of buying a pig in a poke. To buy successfully at a sale requires very sound judgement.

People often feel cautious about approaching a dealer, but, in a business where reputations can be lost on one misdeal, a good name has to be earned and many dealers are fair and reputable. It may not be the cheapest way to buy a horse, but then the dealer is a businessman, and he is likely to allow you to take the animal on trial for a few days on the proviso that if it is unsuitable he will either return your money or exchange the animal. Always choose a reliable and long-established dealer, tell him exactly what you want, and he will usually try to find something to suit your needs and your purse.

## Defects and faults to avoid

When it comes to looking at a prospective purchase, ask to see it both stood up and run out on a hard surface before examining it more closely for defects or signs of possible injury or unsoundness. As it is well worth the expense of getting a veterinary surgeon to check the animal over thoroughly before finalizing the purchase, your own examination need only be to identify any obvious faults which would immediately render the animal unsuitable and therefore save you an unnecessary vet's bill. The horse should stand four-square and evenly, and any inclination to keep resting one leg should arouse suspicions of soreness or strain therein although the horse may not actually be lame. It should be run out in hand on a hard level surface as it is sometimes difficult to detect slight lameness on uneven ground. Shuffling or restricted action may again suggest soreness, while white marks on the insides of the hoofs, slight injuries to the lower leg or unevenly worn shoes can confirm the defective action which will be apparent when the horse is trotted away from you in a straight line.

As the legs are of such vital importance in a driving horse, check them carefully for any heat or swelling including puffy or bowed tendons by running a hand slowly down each leg in turn. Splints, which are bony growths joining the splint bone to the cannon bone, are sometimes found, usually on the inner side of the foreleg, and while they may cause lameness as the enlargement is developing, they rarely cause problems once they have formed

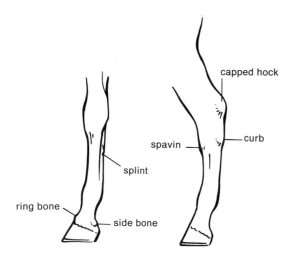

*Fig. 1* Faults and defects in the legs

unless they interfere with the joint **(Fig. 1)**. As such, they are usually of little consequence in a mature horse. Ringbone, which takes the form of a bony enlargement on the pastern can be caused by injury or concussion, in the same way as splints, are or may be hereditary, and horses with this condition should be avoided. The same applies to sidebone, a condition more usually found in horses of draught type, when one or more of the lateral cartilages ossify, causing the hoof wall at the coronet to bulge **(Fig. 1)**.

Windgalls, which are small soft swellings that can appear anywhere between the fetlock joints and the knees or hocks, are a sign of hard work and they are not uncommon in driving horses, which do most of their work on the roads or on hard ground. As they rarely cause lameness, their presence can be read as an indication of excessive concussion, and a lighter workload together with massage or even a short rest will usually overcome them.

Another minor defect caused by strain is thoroughpin which is a distension of the synovial sheath at the back of and just above the hock. Like windgalls, thoroughpin rarely causes lameness and the swelling will often subside with rest or massage.

Curbs and spavins must both be regarded as a weakness although they may not impair the performance of the horse in any way **(Fig. 1)**. A curb is a thickening of the ligament immediately below the hock and is generally caused by over-exertion and strain. Early treatment usually produces a cure with little difficulty, but many horses with pronounced curbs never suffer a day's lameness and continue regular work into old age. Spavins come in two forms, both of which are found on the inside of the hock joint and are the result of strain **(Fig. 1)**. Quite frequently only one hock is affected so the enlargement can easily be detected by comparison, and lameness is not always present. A bone spavin is a hard and bony enlargement, whereas a bog spavin takes the form of a soft swelling. Treatment is possible, although it is not always necessary.

Capped hocks and elbows are unsightly swellings most often caused by regular contact with hard surfaces such as a bare patch of floor in the stable or even the horse's own shoes when lying down **(Fig. 1)**. Insufficient bedding in a concrete-floored loosebox is the most common culprit. The swelling can sometimes be reduced with treatment but, being a cosmetic defect only, it can be overlooked in a horse used only for pleasure driving and not serious showing.

Hoofs should be examined for any signs of 'ridging' around the wall, which might indicate that the horse has had laminitis at some time, and cracks in the hoof wall should be scrutinized carefully. A crack emanating from the coronet and known as a sandcrack can be difficult and expensive to remedy in terms of time and veterinary bills, whereas a crack starting from the ground surface will grow out eventually. Correct maintenance of the hoof by a skilled farrier will hasten the healing process.

Lack of condition may be the result of many things including the serious vices of crib-biting, wind-sucking and weaving, which should be avoided at all costs. Abnormally worn down teeth can be a clue to the former vice, and badly chewed stable fittings and doors will usually verify it. Incorrect feeding, poor grazing and internal parasites can be more innocuous causes of poor condition, and can be easily remedied. External parasites like lice are very easily dealt with but a rubbed, sparse or patchy mane and tail could be the result of sweet-itch, an irritating skin condition to which some horses are prone and which can be difficult to cure. Running a hand slowly down the horse's neck and over its withers, back and loins should reveal any lumps, swellings, heat or injuries which may need more detailed examination.

## Age

A knowledgable person will be able to verify the horse's age by looking at its teeth, but if there is any uncertainty or doubt the matter should be referred to the professional skill of a veterinary surgeon.

## Sound in wind

A driving horse must be sound in its wind. Standing in the stable, its breathing should be noiseless, steady and even, as audible respiratory sound usually points to affectations of the nose, throat or lungs. Quickened breathing could be due to a chest infection, and double breathing with two quite distinct expirations could mean that the horse is broken-winded. Any suspicions in this area should again be referred to a vet.

## Nature and manners

Note how the horse behaves in its box and while being handled and harnessed up, and ask to see it driven before taking the reins yourself. Manners are even more important in a driving horse than a riding horse: the driver is farther away from the horse and the only aids at his or her disposal are the reins, voice and whip, which is why correct basic training is so essential. While it may be argued that manners are taught, there are some faults that are less easily dealt with than others and these are usually directly related to the temperament or nature of the horse. A fear of traffic is a serious problem as a horse which is nervous of motor vehicles is never safe to drive on the roads. Careful and sympathetic schooling can do much to accustom a horse to traffic and give it confidence but, as this can take a long time to achieve and never fully guarantee the horse's behaviour, an animal which is not traffic proof should be eliminated from further consideration.

## Serious vices

Probably the worst fault in a driving horse is kicking and any animal so disposed is potentially dangerous between shafts. Often a horse that kicks frightens itself when its hoofs make contact with the vehicle and it gets out of control or may even bolt with disastrous results. As a kicker generally does so as a defensive action, it is likely that, if put into a situation that is threatening or uncertain, the horse will kick almost as a reflex action although at all other times it may be quiet and reliable in harness. Rearing is equally objectionable as a horse that rears and then topples over backwards can cause very serious harm to both the people in the vehicle and to itself. True bolters are fortunately very rare and invariably suffer from a mental disorder that makes them unpredictable and totally irrational, and therefore a liability in any situation. Horses, which because of inadequate training, incorrect harnessing or careless driving, get out of control and run away are not the same as confirmed bolters but, having done it once are liable to do it again, and can be equally dangerous. Continual shying can be for a number of reasons. Sometimes the problem is caused by ill-fitting blinkers but more usually it is just inexperience combined with fresh-ness on setting out for a drive and many young horses shy. If persistent, the problem may be attributable to defective vision.

## Trial period

If at all possible, take the horse for a short trial period. perhaps a week, to see if it is up to your expectations and requirements. Make allowances for the fact that the horse is in strange surroundings and being handled by people it does not know, and don't make any judgements until it has had a day or two to settle down. If at the end of the trial period the horse has shown itself suitable for the work you require of it, and if you feel the horse is right for you and it has passed the veterinary examin-ation, then the only thing left to do is agree on the price. If the vendor is giving up driving or changing to a larger or smaller driving horse or even progressing to a pair, it may be possible to purchase the harness and vehicle the horse has been driven in previously. This could benefi-cially influence the buying price. Buying a complete turnout is often, though not always, cheaper than purchasing the horse, vehicle and harness separately. Other incentives, like free delivery, could help to ease the negotiating process.

## SUMMARY

***When viewing a horse as a prospective purchase:***
- Meet it in the stable or field as this can be a good indicator of temperament
- See it both stood up and run out on a hard surface
- Check it over carefully for defects or injuries
- Watch it being harnessed and put to the vehicle
- Ask to see it driven before driving it yourself
- See it driven in traffic

***People new to driving are advised to:***
- Go on a driving course or have some lessons before purchasing a driving turnout
- Avoid young or inexperienced horses in preference to 'schoolmasters'
- Take a knowledgeable driving person with you when looking at horses, vehicles or harness

***When choosing a driving horse, make sure it is:***
- Suitable for the intended purpose
- Sound and free from vice
- Traffic proof
- Quiet and well mannered at all times
- Possible to negotiate a trial period

# 2
# BREAKING A HORSE TO HARNESS

The process by which a horse is trained to go in harness can be broken down into a series of related stages, each of which must be fully mastered before moving on to the next. As some horses learn faster than others, and because it is important not to progress until a satisfactory standard has been achieved for each stage, it will take longer to break some horses than others. Most horses will go in harness if correctly trained, the exceptions usually due to bad handling rather than some fault in the horse itself.

## The Horse's Mental Attributes

Whilst breaking a horse is a skilled and specialist job, basic common sense and patience are valuable assets, which can help to compensate for a lack of extensive experience when it comes to putting an animal between shafts. It is also useful to try to understand the nature and mentality of a horse before we begin as it can give us an insight into why horses react to certain situations in the way they do, which in turn can help us to overcome any difficulties or problems that may be encountered. By drawing up a training programme with the mental attributes of the horse in mind, the actual learning process can be considerably simplified.

## Memory

One of the horse's principle mental attributes is its memory, which enables it to recall places or incidents going back over a considerable period of time. For example, a horse properly taught to be tied up as a foal will never forget that lesson for the rest of its life, and will tie up when required thereafter without struggling to break loose. This is because it remembers its initial tying up lessons and is now trained to believe it cannot get loose even though in reality this may not be the case. Similarly, a man could not possibly have the strength to hold a driving team of four strong horses if they decided to run away and it is only because they have been schooled to believe the man is stronger than them, and their memory practices that belief, that makes them controllable. The negative side of memory is that a horse will also always remember bad experiences, with consequential results. A horse that has had a bad fright when travelling in a horsebox or trailer will often be difficult to load again, which shows that he not only remembers the bad experience but that he imagines something similar may happen again. Further evidence of a horse's thought and his imagination, another important mental attribute of the horse which must affect how we train him, is shown when he shies at a stationary object like a paper sack in a roadside, which he evidently imagines has the potential to jump up and harm him or which may conceal something which could do likewise. As the horse is by nature a herd animal whose protection from danger lies in escape by running away, the confidence to face objects that may frighten him must be developed though training, and the presence of an older placid horse in the early stages of breaking can have a quietening effect on a nervous youngster.

### Reasoning

Despite his excellent memory and active imagination, a horse has very poor powers of reasoning and this influences his ability to understand and assimilate our training. If he does wrong, he should be disciplined immediately as even a short lapse of time between error and punishment will disconnect the two incidents in his mind, allowing the former to pass unnoticed and the latter to serve no purpose whatsoever. This is why it is imperative to ensure that the horse understands what we want him to do at all times.

### Observation

A horse's sense of observation is very sharp and stems from the need to be aware of predators or possible dangers in the wild. Something different in the stable yard or out on a familiar exercise route will be noticed and will make him wary.

### Judgement

A horse is also capable of making judgements, as sometimes shown by animals which quickly assess the weaknesses of an inexperienced or nervous rider or driver and behave accordingly by trying to assert their own will in some way.

## The Stages of Training

People planning to drive a riding horse they already own have an initial advantage in that they will know the horse and how he is likely to react in most circumstances. In addition, the horse, being familiar with the owner, will have more confidence than he would if handled by strangers. Nevertheless, familiarity should not lead to contempt and the training process should not be hurried on the premise that as the horse has always been quiet to ride he is sure to be equally quiet to drive.

### Basic handling

For those who are starting from scratch with a young horse, basic handling is very important. Being taught to tie up and lead teaches the horse restraint and control, while regular handling instills confidence and accustoms the horse to having his feet lifted, being loaded and unloaded into horseboxes, and other everyday procedures. As a young horse is very impressionable and receptive to learning, the sooner he can be carefully introduced to traffic the better. An ideal way is to turn him out, preferably with a quiet companion, in a field bordering a busy road but, failing this, lead him on a regular basis down to a busy road and let him watch the traffic from a safe distance so that he does not feel threatened by it. A wide grass verge, gateway or quiet side road is usually adequate for the purpose.

### Bitting and mouthing

Mouthing a horse and accustoming him to having a bit in his mouth and teaching him to respond to it is a vital lesson as the reins constitute the most important of the driver's three aids, the other two being voice and whip in order of importance. A

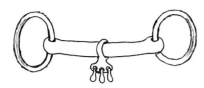

*Fig. 2* Breaking bit with keys

breaking bit with keys **(Fig. 2)** should be used as these encourage the horse to play with the bit, and the mouthpiece should be smooth and thick with no wear evident at the ends where the rings pass through, as looseness can pinch the corners of the mouth. Using a jointed bit in the early stages allows the tongue more room for movement but replacing this with a bit with a straight mouthpiece for long-rein-ing and subsequent work under saddle or in harness avoids the nutcracker action jointed bits exercise. First lessons with a bit in the horse's mouth should be fairly short; no longer than half an hour, increasing to an hour after about a week.

A daily lesson is essential for continuity of training, as a horse learns by repetition. Leave the horse loose in his stable with the bit in but keep an eye on him all the time and make sure there is nothing he can hook the bridle or cavesson on, like a manger or bucket holder, which would frighten him and could make him headshy. Great care should be taken both putting the bridle on and taking it off so as not to catch the bit on his teeth. This can be easily achieved by slipping a thumb into the side of his mouth in the gap where the bit lies, which will cause him to open his mouth. When the bridle is correctly fitted, the bit should just wrinkle the corners of his mouth. If it is too low, and especially if a jointed bit is used, there is the risk of him discovering the irritating habit of getting his tongue over the bit which can cause serious problems later on, but buckling the bit too high up in the mouth will cause him unnecessary discomfort. The bit must

not be too long in the mouthpiece so that slips from side to side, nor so short that it presses on the sides of his mouth.

### Introduction to a roller

After about a week of daily mouthing, the roller can be quietly slipped on and buc-kled up. An assistant must be present to hold the horse while this is done as many young horses arch their backs, buck or kick out as they feel it grip, especially if it is fastened too tightly. It is only necessary to fasten the roller tight enough to prevent it moving should the horse object actively, but a loose roller is dangerous as it can slip to one side, frightening the horse. Some trainers advocate the use of fixed side-reins as soon as the horse has accepted the feel of a roller on his back but, as side reins can impose a restriction for which the horse is neither mentally nor physically ready, the result can often be an overbent animal which fails to accept the bit pro-perly. A young horse's head carriage can-not successfully be improved by artificial means; only when he has learned to go forward with impulsion and with his hocks well underneath him will his head naturally come up into the desired place.

A tie-back comprising a length of thin cord tied by means of elastic rubber loops to the side of the roller and running through the bit rings to the other side of the roller can accustom the horse to the feel of slight pressure on the bit and will encourage him to 'mouth'. The cord should be sufficiently loose that his head movement is not restricted when he is standing normally, and the elasticity of the rubber will prevent him leaning on the bit. Five centimetre (2in) cross sections cut from an old inner tube like large elastic bands are ideal for the purpose. By passing the cord through the bit rings rather than attaching it to them, sideways movement of the head is not restricted.

The horse can be left at liberty in his loosebox to become accustomed to the bridle and roller, or turned out in an enclosed school or small paddock, but constant supervision is important at all times.

## Lungeing

Lungeing is invaluable as a training exercise as it teaches the horse obedience and helps him to achieve suppleness and balance, and it is the ideal medium for familiarizing him with the various parts of a driving harness. An indoor school or all-weather outdoor manège away from distractions is the most suitable place to lunge a horse as it helps concentrate the horse's mind but, failing this, a quiet and level corner of a field can be perfectly adequate if a perimeter boundary of hurdles or oil drums with poles on top is erected. A lungeing cavesson with a webbing lunge-rein attached to the noseband under the horse's chin and a lungeing whip is all that is needed. If a breaking cavesson is not available, an alternative is to pass a length of strong cord through the offside bit ring, over the poll, and back through the nearside bit ring where it is knotted back onto itself under the jaw. A horse should never be lunged directly from the bit. A roller is not essential at this stage and side-reins or tie-backs should never be used on the lunge as we want the horse to stretch his head and neck down to balance himself as he works on a circle. Lungeing is quite hard work for a young horse and lessons should be kept short. The animal should be worked equally on both reins at a walk and at a steady trot, using clear and consistent verbal commands which he will learn to recognize and respond to. The usual commands are 'walk on', 'trot', 'whoa' and 'steady', and these same commands will be used later when he is being driven in harness.

For the first few lessons, an assistant is necessary to lead the horse around the lungeing ring until he understands what is required. The trainer should walk in a small circle, slightly behind the horse, rather than stand in the middle of the ring and turn on the spot. To lunge anti-clockwise, the rein should be held in the left hand with the whip in the right and pointing towards the ground. Always lunge to the left first as most horses go more willingly in that direction because they are used to being led from the near-side. To change direction, stop the horse by giving him the appropriate verbal command reinforced by a steady even pull on the rein to bring him to a halt on the circle. Although the horse may turn his head towards you, he should not be permitted to come into the centre of the ring or he may begin to use this as an evasion, and a driving horse must learn to stand unattended. Quietly reverse the position of the rein and whip and set him off again by moving behind him and telling him to 'walk on'. Young horses new to lungeing sometimes try to swing around to go anti-clockwise again so be prepared for this by positioning yourself slightly behind him and drawing the whip across the ground after him, but without hitting him, to send him forward. The lunge whip should always be used discreetly to keep the horse moving quietly forward or, by pointing it at his shoulder, to keep him out on the track if he is hanging in towards the centre. Maintain a light, even contact on the lunge rein and be careful not to get in front of the horse at any point as this is likely to cause him to stop and turn in to face you. If he tries to race off around the lungeing ring, encourage him to slow down by repeating 'steady' in a quiet voice and just wait until he drops back into a trot at which point give him the command to 'trot' so that he has in effect failed to disobey you. He will soon learn that he cannot go anywhere on the lunge and will settle to his work. Aim to have him working quietly and confidently in both directions at walk and trot with crisp transitions in response to your verbal commands, and use the whip to supplement your voice if he is not paying attention or shows signs of resistance.

## The driving pad and crupper

After a couple of days, the roller can be replaced with a driving pad and crupper. As most animals dislike the feel of a crupper, it is advisable to leave him in the loosebox with it on for a little while before taking him into the lungeing ring. He is still quite likely to object strongly by

clamping his tail down and kicking, which is a natural reaction but he must be made to go forward regardless. Once acceptance of the crupper has been established, the back band, belly band and tugs can be fixed to the pad, and the breeching put on with the breeching straps buckled by means of leather extensions to the tugs to prevent the breeching from sliding up over his back should the horse start to kick. In due course, the collar, hames and traces can be put on, with the latter slipped through the tugs and coiled around themselves and the breeching straps now buckled through the trace hook slots in the ends of the traces. This will accustom the horse to the feel of breeching pressure on his quarters. It is a good idea to fasten the hame terrets on the collar to the pad terrets with a leather strap to prevent the collar sliding down the horse's neck should he lower his head. Always use an 'open' bridle without blinkers for lunge

*Fig. 3* Before introducing a horse to harness, he must first be obedient on the lunge **a**. He can then be lunged wearing first the driving pad and crupper **b**, breeching **c** and collar **d**

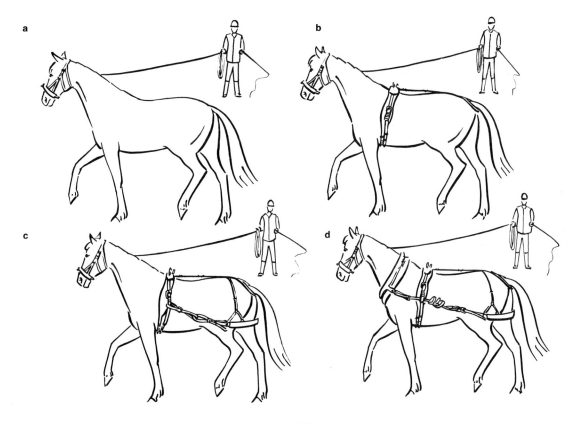

work, and remember that a horse that has been quite happy standing in his stable with harness on may well be frightened by the movement and sound of it when he is trotting on the lunge and make allowances for this by giving him plenty of time to become familiar with the feel of it. For this reason it is advantageous to have the horse obedient on the lunge before the driving harness is introduced **(Fig. 3)**. A horse that has confidence in his trainer and responds to verbal commands is also less likely to be upset by unfamiliar things. Care should be taken to ensure that the harness fits comfortably and does not rub or pinch the horse.

## Long-reining

Long-reining is a very important part of the training process as driving itself is really only an extension of long-reining **(Fig. 4)**. Initially, most trainers lunge the horse using two reins, the inside rein giving direct control while the outside rein lies loosely across the horse's back. If the horse is liable to kick as a result of the outside long-rein across his back and, later, around his quarters a lunge rein to a cavesson will give additional control without interfering with the horse's mouth. It may also indicate that the horse is not ready for this stage of training and more time needs to be spent on the lunge accustoming him to the feel of the harness.

For the first few long-reining lessons, changes of rein should be made by stopping the horse, reversing the position of the reins, then quietly setting him off in the opposite direction by turning his head away from the centre of the ring. As the horse progresses to being driven from behind, as it would be in a vehicle, it should be possible to turn the horse across the school using light even pressure on the inside rein which, as the pressure is transferred to the other rein to complete the

manoeuvre, becomes the outside rein. It is important to ease the rein pressure as soon as a movement is completed and to use the reins in unison, slackening one rein when applying pressure to the other when changing direction or driving figures or circles. As soon as the pupil has got to the stage of being long-reined from behind rather than from the central area of the lungeing ring, the reins can be passed from the bit rings through the shaft tugs on the belly band to the trainer. The reins should never be passed through the terrets on the pad as this minimizes control should the horse play up and can result in the horse swinging around in a circle and knotting the reins. If the reins are passed through the tugs positioned halfway down the sides of the horse and he resists by trying to turn to the left, providing the trainer maintains an even contact on the reins, the horse's quarters swinging out to the right as he turns will put pressure on the right rein, straightening his head and correcting the evasion.

Time spent teaching a horse to long-rein is time well spent. A knowledgable assistant who will, if necessary, lead the horse on in the early lessons is invaluable and, as in all stages of breaking a horse, everything should be done in a quiet, workmanlike manner with the minimum of fuss or impatience. The horse should be taught to walk on, turn in either direction, complete simple figures and halt calmly before being taken out on to the roads to widen his experience.

If satisfactory progress has been made so far, the horse can now be introduced to a blinkered or closed bridle. Blinkers prevent horses being frightened by the sight of moving wheels behind them, the whip being used to give traffic signals, umbrellas being opened, or sudden movements in the vehicle. The pupil should be given plenty of time to get used to blinkers and being long-reined in them, and it is at

Fig. 4 Long-reining is an essential part of a driving horse's education a. An assistant can introduce weight on the traces b before the horse is asked to drag a small sled, log or tyre c

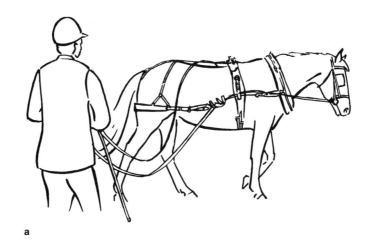

a

b

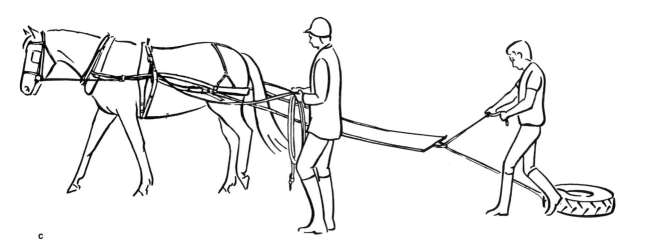

c

this point when the driver can no longer be seen by the horse that the benefits of teaching verbal commands will be realized.

A short period of lungeing before each long-reining lesson is a good idea to settle the horse and re-affirm his basic obedience before progressing onto new ground. One additional lesson worth slipping in when he has reached the standard of lungeing quietly and responsively is to canter him on the lunge with all the driving harness on.

Although cantering on the lunge should not be practised with a young horse, who will find it difficult and may resist as a result, this one exception has a specific purpose as many horses impervious to the harness at walk or trot will react violently by kicking and plunging at a canter.

Horses are always more liable to play up at a canter than a trot and, as it may be necessary to canter him in harness some day when springing a hill or he may break into a few strides of canter himself if something startles him, it is better to sort the problem out now on the lunge than wait until he is between shafts. More time being lunged and long-reined with the harness on will eventually cure any tendencies to misbehave at the canter.

## Learning to pull a weight

The pupil should now be ready to learn to pull a weight. The full set of harness should be put on the horse, with the addition of two lengths of rope which are attached to the trace ends, thereby extending the length of the traces by about 3m (9–10ft). As the horse is driven on the long-reins, an assistant pulls back on the extended traces so that the horse not only has to pull from the collar but also gets used to the feel of the traces against his legs. The assistant should exert a light,

even pressure on the traces at first, gradually increasing the weight until the horse is towing the assistant like a water-skier. For the first lesson, work the horse at a walk only and in large circles or figures, concentrating on getting him to respond to the verbal commands he learned on the lunge while becoming accustomed to the sensation of pulling from his shoulders. In subsequent lessons the assistant can slide the traces up and down the horse's legs and move them sideways so that they press horizontally, and halting and walking on again can be introduced to teach the horse how to pull from a standstill. As the pressure of the assistant pulling back on the traces will not be great, problems are rarely encountered at this stage but it prepares the pupil for the more serious work of pulling an actual weight.

A small, flat sledge on runners, which will pull easily over grass or sand, a log or even an old tyre is ideal, and the traces should be fastened to a swingletree attached to the load with a short length of rope or chain. The purpose of the swingletree is to prevent both traces pulling in against the horse's legs, which might rub or upset him, and the traces should be attached to the swingletree by hooks or some other method, which can quickly and easily be undone if the need arises. A trace bearer over the horse's loins reduces the risk of the horse getting a leg over a trace when turning, which can easily happen when pulling a load from ground level. A tyre has the advantage of being light enough for an assistant to lift off the ground if the horse gets frightened, and quietly lower again when it has calmed down. Some people like to work their young horses in chain harrows prior to being harnessed into a vehicle and, provided the harrows are not too heavy and the horse has some experience of pulling a lighter weight first, this is fine as it accustoms him to noise from behind. An alternative is to have an assistant dragging a chain or pushing a wheelbarrow behind the horse which will serve the same purpose.

Smooth level ground is required for the first lessons in pulling a weight but soon the pupil should progress to working up and down hill, the weight and drag of the load preventing it running forward into the horse's legs on all but the steepest and most slippery of slopes, which should be carefully avoided. Working on inconsistent surfaces like fields, tracks, gravel and the like will accustom the horse to the different sounds the load makes as it drags over different types of ground. Patience at this stage can reap benefits later on in the training.

The breaking bit with which the horse was mouthed at the beginning of his training should have been replaced with a straight-mouthed snaffle, preferably of eggbutt type, for long-reining, but now he should be ready to progress to a proper driving bit in readiness for going between shafts. A Liverpool driving bit with a thick, smooth un-jointed mouthpiece and the reins buckled into the 'plain cheek' position, or a double ring snaffle, should be used. If a double ring or Wilson snaffle is used, the reins should be buckled around both rings on each side of the bit as to buckle the cheek-pieces of the bridle to the floating rings and the reins to the outer rings, as is sometimes seen, exerts extreme pressure, making the bit severe in its action and unsuitable for a young horse.

## An introduction to shafts

The final stage of breaking a horse to drive is to harness him into the vehicle, and this should only be undertaken when the horse has successfully learned all the previous lessons and is obedient to the voice and reins. Some trainers give their horses an introduction to shafts by long-reining them with two thin poles slipped through the tugs and breeching and secured there with little leather straps or string. While there may be some value in using poles in this way, especially with a nervous horse, which benefits from being eased very gradually from stage to stage, they cannot fully imitate the unyielding rigidity of shafts, and need to be fitted and secured with great care. If they project too far forward the horse could catch his bridle on them, and if they are too short the ends could get under the collar, breaking the poles, and any frights caused by such incidents could undo much of the good work already achieved.

## Suitable breaking vehicles

The ideal breaking vehicle is a skeleton breaking cart, a specially built two-wheeled vehicle with a metal bridge over the extra long shafts to carry the reins clear of the horse's back. Unfortunately, such vehicles are now rare and difficult to find, but most strong sound vehicles can be used providing they offer easy access to the driver and are not too heavy. Using a slide-car without wheels has the advantage of being light, inexpensive and easy to construct as it consists only of two long poles for shafts, which drag on the ground at one end and have a platform fastened between them on which a small load can be carried. If the horse gets frightened and tries to take off and has to be turned in a circle to stop him, the vehicle will slide sideways without turning over as a wheeled vehicle might which would really frighten him. Having no wheels, it requires more effort to turn, which is not necessarily a bad thing as it teaches a horse the skill of 'shafting' before he is put into a more expensive vehicle. The big disadvantage of any type of wheel-less breaking vehicle is that it will not slide backwards because the shaft ends would dig into the ground.

Four-wheeled vehicles are not suitable for breaking purposes because if the horse shies suddenly and swings around or tries to run backwards the vehicle would articulate and possibly turn over. Extra long shafts keep a vehicle body out of range of the horse's hoofs in case he should kick, and a low centre of gravity helps to make the vehicle stable. High vehicles with a narrow track width or those where the driver cannot jump on or off easily should be avoided for safety reasons.

## Harness for breaking

The harness must be very strong and supple so that any of the buckles can be undone quickly and easily should the need arise. It is a good idea to check the harness over very carefully before 'putting to' for the first time to ensure that no parts are worn or damaged and that none of the stitching needs renewing. A kicking strap passed loosely over the horse's loins and firmly secured to the shaft on either side to prevent him from getting his hindquarters up should he kick is a wise precaution. If a proper leather kicking strap is not available, a length of strong light rope knotted to the shafts and slipped under the back strap will make a perfectly adequate alternative. A strong headcollar should be worn under the bridle with a lead-rope of at least 2m (6–8ft). One knowledgable assistant is essential to lead the horse, and an additional assistant to help with harnessing and unharnessing is desirable.

## Putting to for the first time

Before being put to for the first time, the horse should be quietly worked to settle it, and it is at this time that the benefits of having a horse broken to ride before it is

driven will be realized. A horse that has been backed after the long-reining phase of training and ridden on to give it a little experience before being driven will be calmer and more receptive in most cases than one for whom going between shafts is its first serious work. If the weather is windy or very wet, it may be prudent to abandon the project until a more favourable day as the horse will never concentrate in adverse conditions, and many horses become noticeably restless in strong winds.

If the horse is uneasy, facing him against a wall to harness him to the vehicle may encourage him to stand, but it also means that he will have to turn as soon as he moves off, which is not always such a good idea. To 'put to', one person should hold the horse by the reins or lead-rope while the other two people quietly bring the vehicle up from behind and slip the shafts through the tugs (**Fig. 5**). Talking to the horse quietly all the time will reassure him, particularly as he will be unable to see the people behind him because of the blinkers, and if the assistants with the vehicle are able to run one hand over his quarters it will prevent him being startled should one of the shafts touch him inadvertently. The vehicle should never be stood with its shafts resting on the ground and an attempt made to back the horse between the shafts as the horse could easily side-step, breaking a shaft and frightening himself. The vehicle should be drawn forward until the tugs are pressed against the tug-stops on the shafts and lying perpendicular with the pad. The traces should be fastened to the tracehooks or swingletree quickly, and the use of strong cord at the trace ends tied in quick release knots may make unharnessing easier, especially if the horse needs to be unharnessed in a hurry.

Some types of American harness have a system whereby the bellyband is wrapped

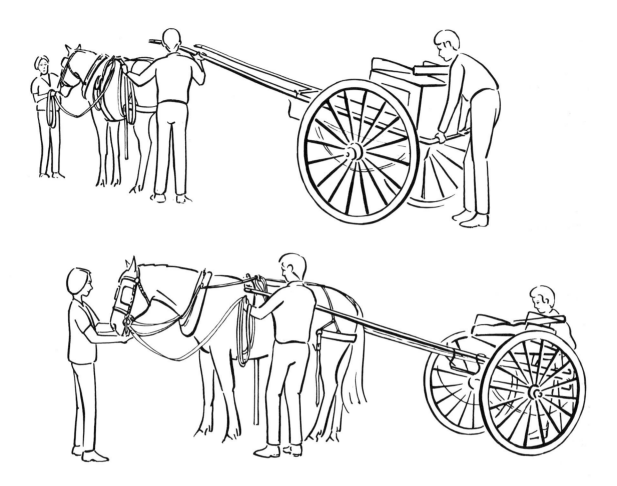

*Fig. 5* Great care must be taken when putting the horse to a vehicle for the first time

several times around the shaft but, because it takes longer to fasten and unfasten than using the open tug buckled onto the backband method, it is best avoided on breaking harness. The belly-band should be buckled fairly tight to prevent the shafts from moving at all as this could easily upset an inexperienced horse.

If a slide-car or some other form of wheel-less vehicle is used, there is no need to use breeching because the vehicle will be unable to run forward into the horse. If, however, the vehicle has wheels, the breeching straps should be buckled around the shafts next so that there is no danger of the vehicle rolling forward and striking the horse's hocks, as nothing is more likely to frighten a young horse and encourage it to kick. Once the horse is harnessed in and everything has been checked over, the driver should take the reins, which for convenience should have been looped through the nearside pad terret to keep them safely out of the way until required, and should position himself on the nearside of the horse and just in front of the vehicle. The assistant, who has been standing in front of the horse to hold him, can now move to stand to the left of and alongside the horse's head, and the other assistant should stand by the offside shaft where they can help by gently pushing or pulling the shaft to left or right to aid the horse in turning the vehicle.

A flat, open field is the most suitable place for these first lessons between shafts as there should be plenty of room to make any turns in wide sweeping manoeuvres. Soft, muddy or sandy ground will substantially increase the effort needed to pull the vehicle, and a firm working surface is preferable. Hills or undulating ground should be avoided for the first few lessons or until the horse has gained a little experience. The lessons should be kept short, no longer than ten or 15 minutes, as the horse can soon tire because he is unaccustomed to the work. Overfacing a horse in terms of the volume or duration of work can lead to resistance and problems, but by dividing the training workload into two short daily lessons the work will be well within the capabilities of the young horse and he will also learn quicker.

## Moving off

When ready to move off, the driver should 'feel' the horse's mouth and give the command 'walk on'. If the horse is facing a wall or hedge, he should be turned to the left, and the assistants should help by easing the vehicle in that direction. If the vehicle is heavier than might be ideal, a little help to get it moving forward will encourage him as moving a deadweight from a halt can sometimes cause young horses to jib. As soon as the horse is walking on, the assistant leading him can give him a little rope by falling back behind his shoulder so that the horse cannot see him and is being controlled solely by the driver although the assistants can quickly step in if needed. At all times the commands the horse learned at the lungeing stage should be used, and if he is frightened or confused, the work should stop and he should be reassured and given time to relax before being quietly set off again.

## Unharnessing the young horse from the vehicle

As much if not more care should be taken unharnessing a horse from a vehicle as putting him to. After a successful lesson, it is easy to become blasé and to fail to observe the mandatory safety precautions. Always halt the horse on level ground, facing a wall if need be, and the assistant should hold him by standing in front of him while the driver loops the reins through the pad terret prior to unfastening the kicking strap, undoing the bellyband, unbuckling the breeching straps and, lastly, unhooking the traces. The vehicle should then be pushed back clear of the horse, which may necessitate another assistant if a wheel-less breaking vehicle is being used. The method of holding the shaft while the horse is led forward out of the vehicle is not recommended as an impatient horse may step forward too soon, causing the shafts to slip out of the tugs and hit the ground and possibly damaging it.

If the horse was started off in a wheel-less vehicle, after a few lessons he should be ready to be put to a wheeled vehicle and, if a proper breaking cart is not available, a flat cart with lengthened shafts makes an excellent alternative. Being low to the ground, a flat cart is very stable and a serviceable breaking model can easily be constructed at home using scrap wood and old car wheels.

The driver has very easy access by sitting on the side of the cart with his legs dangling over the edge. He has to sit sideways to drive, which is uncomfortable and tiring, but the advantages of a flat cart outweigh this failing. However, the drag of car tyres on soft ground as opposed to conventional carriage wheels, which are very narrow in comparison, should always be remembered when planning routes for training drives.

## Driving a young or inexperienced horse

When the horse has got to the stage in his training when he will do in the vehicle what he did in long-reins, the driver can mount the vehicle and this should be done when in motion to accustom the horse gradually to the extra weight. An assistant can join the driver on the vehicle in due course although a 'gypsy line' or lunge-rein from the horse's head to the assistant on the cart is advisable in case of mishaps.

As the length of the drives is increased, the young horse can be taken out on quiet roads and tracks and eventually short periods of slow steady trotting may be introduced. The first kilometre (half mile) or so of each drive should always be driven at a walk so that the young horse learns to set out calmly and without rushing, and the last kilometre home should also be walked so that the horse does not get into the habit of dashing home. If something in the roadside frightens him, it is always better for the assistant to get out and lead him during these early lessons than to risk upsetting him as such incidents will stick in his mind. Hill work needs to be introduced very gradually by accustoming the horse to slight gradients first. Going uphill should present no problems if the horse is not overfaced by being asked to pull too great a weight before he is sufficiently muscled up for the job. He will also find trotting uphill easier than walking because of the extra momentum gained but, as he gains strength and experience, he should not be allowed to lapse into the habit of automatically slipping into a trot as soon as he reaches the bottom of a hill.

The horse also has to learn how to hold back a vehicle on a downhill gradient by decreasing pace and taking the weight of the cart through the breeching. An inexperienced horse faced with a steep downhill slope can be terrified if he feels the breeching is pushing his hind legs from under him, especially on a slippery road surface, and a horse needs to be taught how to breech in easy stages.

By the time the horse is driving out regularly, he should have learned to stand by himself to be harnessed and unharnessed, and he should be ready to go out in company. Initially, he can be driven out accompanied by a ridden horse which should begin by staying in front of him where he can see it then move behind or alongside him. Later, he can be taken out with one or more other turnouts to further his experience.

Only when the horse has been driven for some time and is relatively experienced should he be taught to back or he may use it as an evasion when he does not want to go forward. Also, the horse moves the vehicle by stepping backwards into his breeching so he needs to be fully conversant with how to breech before reining back is taught. Begin by teaching him to back by putting him in long-reins and having an assistant standing in front of the horse. As the driver applies slight pressure on the reins and gives the command 'back,' the assistant pushes the horse back by placing one hand on his muzzle and the other on his chest. When the horse steps back, he should be praised and led forward again. One or two steps are sufficient at first, increasing to about four or five. If the horse resists, the assistant can gently tread on a hoof which will prompt the horse to lift it. Each time he reins back, he should be halted, walked forward and halted again with the appropriate verbal commands as this discourages any inclination to evade the bit by hanging back. When the assistant can be dispensed with and the horse will back in response to the voice and a 'feel' on the reins, the same procedure can be repeated but with the horse harnessed to the vehicle. The assistant should stand by to help if required. The operation can be made easier for the horse if another assistant helps by pulling back on the vehicle the first couple of times, and smooth level ground or even a very slight downhill gradient to the rear of the vehicle will make it roll more easily.

Throughout all the stages of breaking a horse to drive, the essentials are patience, time, and attention to detail, together with calm efficiency on the part of the trainer and his assistants.

## SUMMARY

**When breaking a horse to drive:**
- Never hurry
- Never lose your temper
- Always have an active assistant
- Talk to the horse at all times using clear and consistent commands he can memorize

**When training a young horse, remember he has:**
- An excellent memory
- Poor powers of reasoning
- Sharp sense of observation
- Ability to make judgements

# 3

# SELECTING A HORSE-DRAWN VEHICLE

## Selection Criteria

Choosing a horse-drawn vehicle is not dissimilar from choosing a horse, as many of the selection criteria will be the same. The purpose for which the vehicle will be used, the number of passengers to be carried, the size and type of horse, and the finance available will all have an influence on the final choice.

A primary consideration is whether to opt for a new or an old and original vehicle. The driving revivalists of the 1950s had little choice as there were left in existence very few firms capable of manufacturing new vehicles but, as there were plenty of original vehicles to be found in barns and coach-houses to supply the limited demand, this caused no problems. As driving increased in popularity, fewer old vehicles which were sound and roadworthy became available and it became apparent that there was a rapidly-growing need for craftsmen who could repair and renovate original vehicles as well as build new ones to suit current requirements. The proliferation of new builders in recent years has succeeded in stemming the escalating costs of original vehicles by manufacturing modern examples in large numbers and bringing down the rarity value of horse-drawn vehicles in general.

### New or old?

Old vehicles tend to be more interesting than new ones on account of their individuality. At a time when there were literally thousands of coach-building firms, each one built vehicles to its own particular designs and to suit the specific requirements or whims of the customer, with the result that rarely were two vehicles exactly alike. The outstanding craftsmanship in many old vehicles is of a standard rarely seen in modern vehicles, although there are exceptions, and old vehicles inevitably hold their value better than new examples. In the showring, an old vehicle will inevitably score over a new one as the judging of private driving classes is based on the traditions of the sport and a well-restored antique vehicle is more likely to appeal to the judge than one which is obviously of modern design.

However, an old vehicle is limited in its versatility, as a valuable antique is hardly the most appropriate conveyance to drive in a cross-country marathon or a scurry competition, whereas all-purpose modern vehicles, which successfully meet a range of functions, are now available. The problems of finding a suitable original can involve many fruitless and expensive trips to carriage sales and private vendors before something is found, and restoration, whether done at home or by a professional, can delay getting the vehicle on the road and increase the overall costings. As with anything old, regular maintenance is important to keep an original vehicle roadworthy and looking smart, and any breakages or accidental damage is usually more expensive to rectify than it would be with a new vehicle because of the materials needed and the skill and craftsmanship required to do the job.

New vehicles are now readily available in a wide range of designs and materials, from inexpensive exercise carts with wire wheels and bodies of tubular metal construction, to superb authentic reproductions of traditional carriages using the same materials throughout as were used in the originals **(6, 25, 47)**. Apart from the convenience of being able to order a new vehicle from stock as is the case with many manufacturers, standard spare parts are usually easily obtainable, which keeps the cost of repairs, as well as the time the vehicle is out of commission, to a minimum. As mass production techniques have enabled modern builders to produce cheap and serviceable exercise vehicles in large numbers, the appreciation value of such vehicles will be negligible, and it is only the individually built and expensive copies of original vehicles or specially designed and constructed competition vehicles that are likely to appreciate in value.

Some modern designs have additional benefits like interchangeable wheels and shafts to enable the vehicle to be used for horses and ponies of varying heights. Others incorporate adjustment mechanisms for widening and lengthening the shafts or altering the height of the body for the same purpose. Some new vehicles dismantle completely to facilitate transportation to shows or rallies, and on others the shafts unbolt to be replaced by a complete forecarriage and pole to adapt the vehicle from two wheels to four. The introduction of rigorous new driving competitions, such as combined driving, has created a need for new types of vehicles. Modern materials, including alloys, epoxy resins and fibre-glass, are now used in vehicle manufacture in place of the more traditional wood by some builders, and new developments and innovations are constantly challenging the accepted practices.

### Two or four wheels?

Generally, two-wheeled vehicles are more suitable for driving a single horse to than four-wheelers **(Fig. 6)** as there is no advantage in the extra weight and drag of four wheels and, being more manoeuvrable, a two-wheeler is safer as it cannot articulate and possibly tip over if the horse backs up unexpectedly. A two-wheeler also takes up less room, which may be worth bearing in mind if storage space is at a premium, and is easier to transport for the same reason. To their credit, four-wheeled vehicles can easily be adapted for pair driving, whereas the very few two-wheelers that have provision for a pole need specialized cape or curricle harness, which has its own inherent disadvantages. Although hardly an argument in favour of one or the other, there are no adjustments necessary to balance a four-wheeled vehicle whereas the two-wheeler needs the weight distributing evenly over the axle to ensure that the shafts are neither pressing down on the tugs, nor 'light on' and pointing skyward.

## *Types of Vehicle*

Vehicles suitable for private driving come in an almost-infinite variety, all with quite distinct and differing features, but to aid

*Fig. 6* **a** Stanhope gig and (*below*) **b** Wagonette

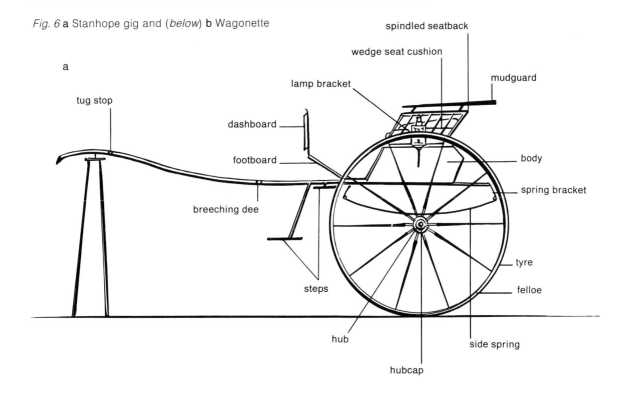

a

spindled seatback

wedge seat cushion

mudguard

lamp bracket

tug stop

dashboard

body

footboard

spring bracket

breeching dee

tyre

steps

felloe

hub

side spring

hubcap

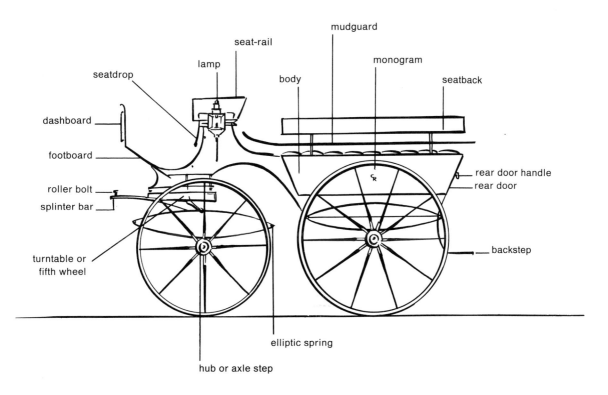

b

mudguard

seat-rail

monogram

lamp

seatback

seatdrop

body

dashboard

footboard

rear door handle

rear door

roller bolt

splinter bar

turntable or
fifth wheel

backstep

hub or axle step

elliptic spring

identification and description most can be roughly divided into a number of broad family groups. Some of the larger four-wheeled carriages like landaus and broughams are coachman-driven and therefore unsuitable for private or owner-driven use, and trade vehicles, like floats, which developed for commercial transportation, are similarly unsuited to pleasure driving.

## Gigs

Gigs (**10**, **13**, **29**, **35**, **39**, **45**, **47**), which comprise one of the largest and most popular groups, evolved from the sedan chair and first made their appearance in England in the late eighteenth century.

The three features that distinguish them from other vehicles are that they are always two-wheeled, they seat the driver and one passenger in a forward-facing position, and the double seat is fixed and does not slide forwards and backwards on runners. The early gigs were very crudely built with little more than a plank for a seat, no springing, and small, heavy wheels, but by the nineteenth century more refined examples were being turned out, and the enormous variety of gigs we know today began to make their appearance. One of the earliest was the rib-chair gig, which had a semi-circular spindle-back seat. However, it was unsprung and very uncomfortable, and was soon superseded by the Tilbury gig, invented and built by Tilbury, the London coach-builder, which over-compensated by having seven springs, making it extremely heavy. The Honorable Fitzroy Stanhope amended the design to produce the gig that still bears his name. It had only four springs but the addition of a boot made it very popular with 'bagmen' or commercial travellers. The shafts on Stanhopes curve

12   Mrs Jennifer Harrison driving her Fell pony, Flash of Tebay, to a gig of modern design

13  Miss Mary Longsden driving her Fell mare, Bewcastle Bouquet, to an original gig built by Mills of London. The straight shafts, which curve where they are attached to the vehicle (to follow the lines of the body), are characteristic of gigs built by Mills

right around the back of the vehicle in a continuous sweep and are plated with iron, which makes these gigs very heavy, and a strong horse is needed between the shafts. Improvements to the Stanhope design gave rise to several other types of gig, including the Dennett, a lighter vehicle with a three-spring suspension system, and the skeleton gig, which has curved brackets to support the spindle-back seat as there is no boot. These elegant and attractive vehicles are excellent for private driving but the open seat-back offers little protection from the weather, and the round-back design of gig, which has a solid, curved panel enclosing the seat may suit all-weather drivers better. Another type of gig, the well-bottom, has a recessed hollow for the driver's feet and legs which keeps the

vehicle lower to the ground, affords easy access, and makes it less likely to turn over.

Liverpool gigs **(10)**, many of them built by the famous coachbuilders, Lawton of London and Liverpool, have stylish panelled bodies and are much favoured in the showring. Some gigs are fitted with leather hoods and called either hooded gigs or 'buggies' although the latter is now really an American term used generically to describe many types of two- or four-wheeled vehicles, hooded or not. The name 'ogee' is sometimes used to refer to the curved shape of the vehicle body, and is often used to describe the elegant lines of some hooded gigs. There are also gigs described by their design as cut-under, cab-shafted or cee-spring.

As the seat in a gig is fixed, the vehicle needs to be constructed so that the driver and passenger sit right over the axle and the unladen weight is evenly distributed in front of and behind the axle so that the vehicle balances perfectly. Although a little adjustment is possible by fractionally moving the axle forwards or backwards on the springs, vehicles which are badly balanced can be very uncomfortable and tiring for both the horse and the occupants of the gig.

## Sulkies

The sulky evolved from the early gigs used for the trotting matches that were very popular in the last century, but modern pneumatic-tyred sulkies bear little resemblance to their large-wheeled ancestors except that they are very light in weight and seat only one person. They are unsuitable for private driving because of the uncomfortable seating arrangement for the driver, who has to rest his feet in metal loops on the sides of the shafts, and their overall design is purely for harness-racing on smooth tracks. Another single-seater is the so-called doctor's gig, a light well-sprung vehicle once favoured by those in the medical profession.

## Whiskies

Yet another off-shoot of the gig is the whisky which has a light, cane-sided body hung on two horizontal springs. Its name came from the speed at which it supposedly whisked along the roads but, sadly, these stylish vehicles are now rare.

## Dogcarts

The dogcart (3, 14, 40) is an indirect descendant of the gig and first made its appearance in the early nineteenth century. Both two- and four-wheeled versions were built but dogcarts differ from gigs in that they can carry four

14 Marsh Shadow, a part bred Arab gelding, driven by his owner, Miss Glenis Dodd, to a dogcart. Originally, these vehicles were designed for carrying sporting dogs under the seat, and the louvred side panels were for ventilation

people instead of two, the double seats being arranged back-to-back with the tailboard letting down on chains to provide a footboard for rear passengers. Their deep boots have slatted sides for ventilation and were used for carrying sporting dogs, hence their name. As two-wheeled dogcarts have a sliding front seat operated by a lever or screw handle, it is possible to adjust the weight over the axle to correct the balance. Some even have a mechanism whereby the whole body can be moved forwards or backwards on metal runners, and balancing adjustments can be made when the vehicle is in motion.

The Parkgate gig, a vehicle of American design, combines many of the features of a gig with the angular shape and louvred sides of a dogcart, and is an ideal vehicle for either single or tandem driving. Specialized types of dogcart include the cocking cart, originally used for transporting fighting cocks, the American 'Going to Cover' cart, and the tandem cart with its high seat. The erroneously named suicide gig of the eighteenth century was really a dogcart, and was so named as the groom's seat was nearly 1m (3ft) higher than the already high driver's seat.

## Ralli Cars

The success of the dogcart gave rise to many other types of vehicle with back-to-back seating of which the ralli car (1, 8, 15, 36, 49), which made its debut at the end of the nineteenth century, is still the most popular. Named after the Greek shipping family of that name, who lived in Surrey, it

15 Mrs Iris Thompson driving her Welsh/Hackney cross pony, Tollymoor Gay Lad, to a ralli car in a dressage competition. Ralli cars are distinguished by the side panels which curve outwards, and some have false louvres on the lower panels like a dogcart

is distinguishable by having side panels that curve out over the wheels to form mudguards, and the shafts usually run inside rather than under or alongside the body. Four-wheeled examples, sometimes referred to as curve-panel phaetons, usually have provision for a pole and splinter bar to be fitted in place of the detachable shafts so that, like four-wheeled dogcarts, they can be used for single or pair driving.

## Country carts

Other descendants of the dogcart include a variety of two-wheeled country carts (5) which, because of their roomy back-to-back seating, are ideal family vehicles for general driving or rallies but equally appropriate for the showring. Some have solid side panels, others are slatted or have rails to reduce the weight, and in some examples the rear seat is removable to give extra luggage space. Often they were named after their county of origin, like Norfolk carts. Other designs include village carts, which seat only two people but have plenty of room under the seat for parcels or other goods. It is customary for country vehicles to be simply varnished rather than painted, although if the vehicle is old and has been repaired with new wood in places it may be difficult to stain the new wood to match the old, in which case painting may be the only sensible solution.

## Governess cars

The governess car is invariably two-wheeled although a few four-wheeled versions were built. It is recognizable by its low, circular or square body with seats on either side, which is entered by a door at the back. Governess cars were built, as their name implies, to be driven by governesses when they took their charges out

for an airing in the park, and their design made it difficult for children to fall out or even reach the handle positioned halfway down the outside of the door. They should be driven from the offside rear corner seat, but their design means that both the driver and passengers are obliged to sit sideways, which can cause discomfort, and a well-mannered horse is essential as the position of the seats limits the driver's control and inhibits easy exit from the vehicle. The governess car is still a distinctive and attractive vehicle, and many fine examples with elegant lines and spindled bodies were turned out by the best city coachbuilders. Basket-sided versions were also produced, and others had side, dennett or even cee-springs in place of the more usual fully elliptic springs. Plainer, solid-sided examples are often referred to as 'tub traps' on account of their shape; the term 'trap' being used generally to describe any two-wheeled vehicle although it originally referred to those vehicles, like governess cars, with poor access in which the driver was literally trapped.

## Princess and Leicester cars

One-off designs, which do not fit easily into any particular group, include the princess car and Leicester car (16). Both resemble a governess car in overall shape except that both are entered from the front on either side of the dashboard as in a gig or dogcart, and have a double seat facing forward which slides on runners to adjust the balance. The princess car has cab shafts and a wide body hung low between elliptic springs on a cranked axle, whereas the Leicester car is a higher vehicle on side springs with two inward-facing seats at the back reached by a door and a step. This seating arrangement is safer and more comfortable for rear passengers than the backward-facing rear seats in dogcarts

**16** Mrs J. Jenner driving her Fell mare, Dalemain Columbine, to a Leicester car. These distinctive vehicles have a rear door giving access to two small inward-facing seats at the back

or ralli cars which are invariably narrow and tipped at an angle to give little security if the horse moves suddenly or if travelling on rough ground.

## Meadowbrooks

One of the most popular American vehicles is the meadowbrook (**9, 17, 33**), a lightweight two-wheeled two-seater, which is entered from the back. The forward-facing and independent seats hinge at the sides to allow access to the front, and one or both seats have hinged backrests, which fold down over the cushion when not in use. Being light and well sprung, they are comfortable, and their low centre of gravity makes them very stable, but the seating arrangement means that the driver has to stand up in order to lift the seat before getting out, which makes the meadowbrook less suited for driving young or difficult horses to.

17  Mr T.W. Fawcett driving a Morgan horse mare to a meadowbrook. The brass gauze upper part of the dashboard is to prevent dirt and small stones being thrown up from the road onto the driver or passenger without obscuring their view of the horse

## Road carts

There are a variety of two-wheeled vehicles that can be classed together under the name of exercise or road carts **(21)**. They are essentially lightweight, utilitarian vehicles comprising little more than shafts, wheels and a double seat facing forward, and they may not even have the refinement of springs if on pneumatic tyres. They can be built of metal, wood or other materials and, being inexpensive, many people choose one when they first take up driving. As they are easy to build, many firms with limited experience of horse-drawn vehicle construction are producing them at low cost and it is important to select one that is well designed and strongly built to withstand the strains of regular use. Many have small, wire-spoked wheels which may buckle easily, and tubular shafts which can bend, and the low seat is not conducive to a good driving position or maximum control of the horse. Far preferable, although more expensive, are those vehicles designed specifically for competitive driving, particularly cross-country marathons, which are robustly built on larger wheels and with a raised seat to give the driver sufficient height together with adequate leg room and purchase for the feet to ensure a secure and effective position. Some also have a broad back step the full width of the vehicle for a groom to stand on and help stabilize the vehicle by moving their weight from side to side when travelling on rough ground or turning at speed.

## Phaetons

Phaetons **(18, 24, 44, 48)** make up the largest group of four-wheeled vehicles and they take their name from Phaeton, the son of Helios the sun god, who according to Greek mythology stole his father's sun chariot and proceeded to lose control of the horses, which bolted towards earth and nearly set it on fire. Apart from always having four wheels, the other identifying characteristics of phaetons are that they are open, owner-driven vehicles seating two or more persons. Early examples were exceptionally high, rather sporty vehicles but later designs showed considerable diversity and variation. George IV phaetons, named after the King, who had one built for use in his later years, have small wheels and low-slung bodies with high dashboards, which curve slightly towards the horse's quarters. Park phaetons, which evolved from them specifically for

18  Mrs Barbara Stothert driving a pair of Welsh Mountain ponies to an American basket-panel phaeton. The back-to-back seating arrangement with the tailboard letting down as a footrest is more commonly found in dogcarts and ralli cars

afternoon drives in the park, are similar, except that the curve of the dashboard is more pronounced and there is often a rumble or small groom's seat on the back. A number are fitted with a folding hood. Smaller park phaetons are often referred to as pony phaetons. The graceful lines of the body and splashboards make these vehicles elegant as well as safe and easy to get in and out of, but the low driving seat is a disadvantage as it restricts visability and limits effective control of the horse.

Although many George IV and park phaetons were designed to be drawn by a single horse or pony, mail phaetons are essentially pair horse vehicles being heavy and solidly built with a hooded boxseat for the driver and passenger and a railed seat behind for use by grooms. Like mail coaches, from which they take their name, they are built with a perch or longitudinal beam between the front and rear axles, forming a foundation for the undercarriage, and telegraph or platform springing adds to the already considerable weight. A lighter version, known as the demi-mail phaeton, has elliptic springs and no perch. The Stanhope phaeton is

smaller and lighter still and has a spindle-back boxseat, which reduces the weight further and enables it to be drawn by a single horse. The T-cart is simply a smaller version of the Stanhope phaeton with the groom's seat reduced in size so that it only seats one, whereas the Beaufort phaeton has an extra seat incorporated so that shooting parties of up to six persons can be accommodated.

Of the many designs of phaeton, the spider phaeton is the most elegant and is acknowledged to be the ideal vehicle in which to display the action of a fine pair of carriage horses. The hooded seat is set upon a pair of arched irons which support a small platform at the back on which a single detachable groom's seat is positioned.

## Wagonettes

The wagonette is classed as a general purpose vehicle suitable for private driving although in the last century, when it was introduced from Germany, it was often coachman-driven. Wagonettes are always four-wheeled, usually hung on elliptic springs, and the body is fitted with seats on both sides. The seats face inwards and are reached by a rear door as with a governess car. There is a raised boxseat for the driver and a passenger.

## Runabouts

Among the distinctly American four-wheelers, one of the most popular is the runabout (19, 46), a multi-purpose vehicle seating two on a forward-facing seat, which is sometimes fitted with a parasol-top to shade the occupants from the sun. The Surrey has the addition of an identical double seat behind the front seat as well as sweeping mudguards that meet at a central step, which they protect from mud thrown up from the road. Many also have a fixed or folding canopy and, like the runabout, surreys have a perch with transverse elliptic springs at either end to provide suspension. A more unique arrangement is used for the buckboard, which has no springs and relies on a single oak plank connecting the front and rear axles to provide some degree of suspension by acting like a spring. The double seat is either built onto the actual board or onto a wooden platform attached to it, giving a surprisingly comfortable ride. Some buckboards have up to three double seats built one behind the other, or a small rumble seat situated between the back wheels. One major disadvantage of many American four-wheelers is that only a limited turning lock can be achieved with the front wheels before they touch the sides of the vehicle or the perch undercarriage. An arch built into the body to accommodate the wheels and referred to as a 'cut under body' is used to increase the lock on some vehicles, but a stationary roller on the perch or on the side of the vehicle for the wheel to turn against reduces the risk of the vehicle jamming and tipping over.

## Choosing a Vehicle

If you are looking to buy an original vehicle or even a second-hand new vehicle, specialist carriage sales are probably the best way of going about finding what you want. Following up advertisements in the equestrian press can be time-wasting and expensive, and carriage restorers and dealers are few and far between and generally highly priced. Sales of vehicles, harness, carriage parts and

19  Messrs G.T. Heard and W. Jones' Welsh Cob stallion, Derwen Rebound, driven to a piano-box runabout. Note the 'clip-on' type American shafts and transverse springs at each end of the vehicle

sundry driving equipment are held regularly on both sides of the Atlantic and bargains can sometimes be picked up although, on the other hand, it is easy to get carried away with the excitement of an auction and bid higher than you intended. Sales are also no indication of market values as two keen bidders can inflate the price for an item out of all proportion. Checking through the catalogue prior to the sale will probably identify a few vehicles, which from their descriptions may be suitable, but go to the sale with a tape measure and a note of the shaft height, width and length that fit your horse as appearances can be very deceptive and costly in the long run. When a two-wheeler is correctly 'put to' the floor of the vehicle should be absolutely level, and the shafts should sit lightly in the tugs when the vehicle is loaded. Some vehicles may appear badly balanced unloaded but be fine when people are in and seated, or vice versa, but this can easily be put to the test by getting someone to stand between the shafts and hold them near the tug stops

while someone else gets into the vehicle and sits down. With vehicles that have no integral balancing arrangement like a sliding seat, this is of vital importance. The shafts should be wide enough to accommodate the horse, which might otherwise suffer from rubbed sides, and long enough so that the shaft tips are about level with the hames on the collar. If they are too short, they may slip between the horse's shoulders and the collar, and if too long, there is the danger of getting a rein caught on the end or even of the horse banging his nose on the shaft tip when turning. Most importantly, there must be adequate room between the horse's hindquarters and the dashboard to avoid any risk of rubbing his tail or, more seriously, the vehicle touching his hocks when in motion. The height of the vehicle can be altered a few inches by the addition or removable of hardwood blocks between the axle and the springs, and it is important to check that a vehicle does not already have blocks in place already raising it to maximum height (Fig. 7).

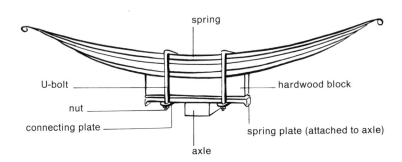

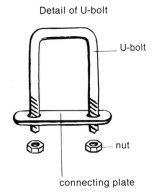

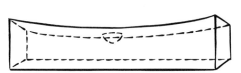

hardwood block showing shaped upper surface to fit tightly against spring (drilled centre recess to accommodate bolt and nut holding spring leaves together)

*Fig. 7* Fitting a wooden block to raise vehicle height

## Shafts

Shafts were traditionally made of lancewood, ash, or sometimes hickory, and shaped according to the style of the vehicle and the fashion at the time. Lancewood is a straight-grained, springy but brittle wood that used to be imported from the West Indies. Although it can be slightly bent for making curved shafts, this weakens it, and lancewood shafts on an original vehicle can usually be identified by their fineness, flexibility and straightness. If damaged they tend to splinter. Ash shafts have much less spring and are usually heavier and thicker but they can be bent to quite exaggerated shapes. In recent years, laminated ash shafts, made from layers of wood glued together, have been produced: they are strong, springy and receptive to being shaped without losing any resilience.

Four-wheeler shafts are usually made from ash as flexibility is unnecessary and would serve no purpose. Check wooden shafts very carefully for cracks, especially around the tug stops and tips, and for unsoundness or breaks at the point where they are attached to the vehicle. Breaks are usually repaired with the aid of a metal plate rebated into the underside of the shaft. They can be easily detected, but damage to the shaft ends, often caused by dropping the shafts, is sometimes hidden by the protective and decorative patent leather sleeve. Fibre-glass shafts are strong and flexible, but metal shafts have virtually no 'give' in them at all and can be unduly heavy. Some vehicles have a small, curved spring to attach the rear end of the shaft to the body, and others have a transverse leaf spring at the front to which the shafts are bolted to increase flexibility. The latter is especially useful if the vehicle has short cab shafts that finish at the dashboard. Lastly, check to make sure the shafts are actually a pair as sometimes one shaft gets broken and is replaced by another of slightly different shape or length or even a different type of wood, which may affect the balance and ride of the vehicle.

## Wheels

Wheels are generally built to one of three designs: staggered, Warner or wedge. The first are so-named because the spokes are staggered where they fit into the hub and, although this arrangement is durable and strong, it demands that the hubs are fairly large and cumbersome. The Warner design incorporates a metal collar that fits tightly around the smaller and neater hub and secures the spokes, which are all level with each other. The wedge wheel has no proper hub at all, and the spokes are tapered at their hub ends so that they fit side-by-side around the axle box and are held in place between two metal discs, which are integral parts of the box casting. The spokes are driven so tightly together in the groove between the discs that no movement is permitted. The design was so extensively used by the army that they are now also known as 'artillery' wheels. Metal wheels that have the spokes welded into the felloes and hub lack the elasticity of wooden wheels, but improvements in the design and manufacture have resulted in wheels that are very strong and have the appearance of traditional wooden wheels. Aluminium and epoxy resin hubs have been experimented with, and roller bearings are now standard on virtually all modern wheel hubs. Traditional coachbuilders used several types of wood for wheel manufacture, notably oak for the spokes and hubs, and ash, which was sometimes steam bent, for the felloes. Hickory was also much favoured by American wheelwrights.

Dished wheels are shaped so that the spokes slope outwards slightly from the hub and are fitted to an axle tree such that the spokes below the hub remain vertical while the spokes above the hub slope outwards. A dished wheel puts less strain on the wheel nuts thereby reducing the risk of the wheel coming off and, as the top of the wheel is further from the vehicle body without altering the track width, less dirt is thrown up onto the vehicle.

## Tyres

Although metal tyres are very hard wearing, they are also extremely noisy on the road, and rubber tyres are a much better option for general driving, the exception being for cross country marathons where sharp turns in ruts and muddy conditions can literally pull off a rubber tyre. Some rubber tyres are held in place in the metal channel that goes around the felloe by wires, which run through the rubber and are welded together before the ends of the tyre are pressed together to close the gap. As the wires can rust through, this method is not perfect, and the clencher system whereby the solid rubber tyre is gripped in position by the pincher-shaped channel is much more secure. Badly-worn tyres or those with gaps where the ends join can necessitate the services of a professional wheelwright, and an unevenly-worn tyre can indicate a buckled wheel, which may need to be rebuilt. A loose tyre can sometimes be replaced by tapping it carefully back into the channel using a hammer and a blunt chisel. Check that the wheels are a true pair and not unequally dished due to one tyre being put on too tightly. Spinning the wheel on the axle will show up warped or buckled wheels.

## Axles

Vehicles with wheels attached to the axle using a simple linch pin system can usually be dated prior to 1840 and as such

as more likely to be in a museum than on the roads and in regular use. More usually, the wheels are held on by the collinge system, which has a longitudinal oil groove running the full length of the axle tree. A leather washer, a collet, and two nuts, which tighten on opposing threads with a split pin through the end of the axle tree, secure the wheel, and this method has never been improved upon as it is safe and requires less frequent greasing of the axle than any other system. Alternatively, the wheels may be held on by the mail box method, which consists of a revolving metal plate secured at the top of the axle tree through which three bolts driven through the hub of the wheel pass and are bolted so that the plate turns with the wheel. The disadvantage of the mail box system is that the wheels need to be regularly removed to grease the axle and this causes wear on the bolt threads, apart from being time consuming.

If a wheel is loose on the axle and can be shaken backwards and forwards, this can easily be fixed by replacing the thin or worn out leather washer at the top of the axle tree with a new, thicker one. The size of the wheels should be in relation to the size of the vehicle but it should be remembered that, whilst the smaller the wheel the stronger it is likely to be as less leverage can be exerted on the spokes, larger wheels are less affected by obstructions or holes in the road and consequently give a smoother and easier ride.

Check carefully for any unsoundness around the felloes, as this is where any rotten wood is usually found on a wheel although often only that part of the felloe which has been in contact with the ground when the vehicle was stored is affected. Thick, cracking paintwork or uneven surfaces may conceal areas of rotten wood that have been filled with putty or fibreglass. Loose spokes can sometimes be remedied by soaking the whole wheel in water for about twenty-four hours to allow the wood to expand as too dry a storage place can cause wheels to dry out and shrink.

## Suspension

The suspension systems used on vehicles vary according to the age, style and purpose of the vehicle but, with the exception of a few early examples, most have some form of leaf springing appropriate to their design. Governess cars, for example, are usually suspended on fully elliptic springs whereas this style of suspension is uncommon in gigs or dogcarts. The particular style is of less importance than the condition and effectiveness of the springs, which should be examined carefully for leaves that are broken or out of alignment, badly rusted, pitted or worn. Also check for signs of wear on the shackles or, in the case of cee-springs with leather suspension straps, rotted stitching or cracks in the leather. A few vehicles were built with lancewood or whalebone springs but these are now very rare. Some modern competition vehicles are fitted with indispension units, telescopic springs or shock absorbers, which are often very effective for the type of driving these specialist vehicles are built for, but unsightly. Vehicles with hard springing give a jarring and rough ride, whereas very soft springing is equally uncomfortable due to the constant bouncing and swaying of the vehicle.

## Bodywork

Rotten or defective woodwork is the main fault to check for in relation to the bodywork, although excessive woodworm damage in an unrestored vehicle can also be cause for concern. Surface rust on metal fittings like lamp brackets or steps can be dealt with easily, but serious corrosion can weaken supporting iron-work. Deep cracks in the side panels or tailboard may be difficult to rectify, and unsound areas in steam bent or shaped bodywork can be very expensive to renew. Look carefully for signs of 'filling', particularly along the bottom of side panels or anywhere else where water could have collected if the vehicle was badly stored.

Fibre-glass bodies should have no unsoundness problems and scratches can easily be polished out using a fine abrasive liquid, but metal bodies, apart from rust damage, can suffer metal fatigue due to the rigidity of the material when subjected to excessive stress. The condition of leather dashboards, mudguards or hoods on those vehicles which have them should be noted, as renewing such items can be prohibitively expensive, and the condition of the upholstery should be checked.

Shafts are best attached to the outside of the body as integral shafts which pass through holes in the footboard and run along the inside of the body tend to produce vibration if the vehicle is not perfectly balanced. Similarly, lamp brackets are better if fitted to the sides of the body out of the way, rather than to the dashboard where they can catch the reins or be an impediment when people are getting in or out of the vehicle. A swingletree giving direct draught from the axle, or trace hooks fitted to short leaf springs on the front of the vehicle are preferable to trace hooks screwed onto the shafts. Many four-wheeled vehicles, and a few two-wheelers, have brakes operated usually by a hand lever with a ratchet device or occasionally by a foot pedal. A brake on a four-wheeler is very useful, especially on a hill if the vehicle is loaded, but on a two-wheeler the result of applying the brake is to pivot the weight of the body on the axle causing it either to press down on the tugs or up on the bellyband. Traditional brakes apply a wooden block to the tyres but modern disc or drum brakes are too severe for spoked wheels unless carefully adjusted and can easily lame a horse in the shoulder or damage the wheels if forcefully applied.

## Paintwork

At one time, vehicles for town use were painted, and vehicles for country use were just varnished natural wood but modern day practicality has outdated such traditions. One advantage on an old vehicle, which has been restored to a natural wood finish, is that it is difficult to hide new wood or filling under a transparent layer of varnish, whereas several layers of paint can hide a multitude of faults. Badly-restored vehicles, which have been amateurishly painted and lined should be regarded with caution. Discreet colours like navy, dark green, maroon or black are preferable to garish colours, although black and yellow or black and red are quite acceptable for sporting vehicles like dogcarts. Lining the wheels, shafts and springs in a contrasting colour can lighten the appearance of a vehicle but excessive lining can look gaudy and distracting, and the body should not be lined at all. Varnished vehicles should also not really be lined although some owners like a little lining on the springs to make them appear more elegant.

The upholstery should be in a hard-wearing material like Melton cloth or Bedford cord, and of a colour in keeping with the paintwork. Fawn is a favourite as it shows the dirt less than some colours and goes well with any colour scheme. Patterned materials or figured fabrics like brocade are incorrect. Fittings on the shafts, the whip-holder **(Fig. 8)** and any beading around the bodywork should preferably be brass rather than nickel and should match, although turned wooden whip-holders can also look very attract-

ive. Many old vehicles have the builder's name engraved on the hubcaps but, as these were sometimes removed and changed around, such information cannot be relied upon.

The descriptions of vehicles in sale catalogues usually give the prospective buyer an intimation of what to expect ranging from 'requiring restoration' suggesting structural repairs as well as repainting and reupholstering, to 'show condition' meaning finished to a very high standard and suitable for exhibiting in shows. In between there will be vehicles in original condition perhaps just requiring repainting, and others with paintwork which is sound but more protective than decorative.

## Balance and legroom

Apart from actually sitting in a vehicle to ensure that it balances if it is a two-wheeler, it is worth getting in to see if there is sufficient leg room, that the driving seat is high enough, and that the vehicle is easy to get in and out of. An adjustable footrest **(Fig. 9)** can help if the footboard is too far away, and an extra cushion or a shaped 'wedge' seat can give more height if required **(29)**.

## Building your own vehicle

For those ambitious enough to want to build their own vehicle, the advantages and disadvantages need to be objectively weighed up as little, if anything, will be saved financially and the involvement in terms of time can be very considerable. Commercial horse-drawn vehicle manufacturers using mass production techniques on tried and tested designs can produce vehicles under factory conditions with all the benefits of bulk buying, standard component parts and conveyor belt assembly to keep the price down to a

*Fig. 8* Whipholder

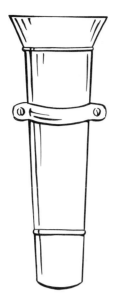

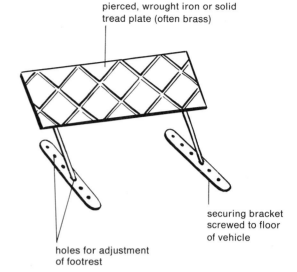

pierced, wrought iron or solid
tread plate (often brass)

securing bracket
screwed to floor
of vehicle

holes for adjustment
of footrest

*Fig. 9 (Far right)*
Adjustable footrest

minimum. For the amateur vehicle builder, the cost of the wheels, axle, springs and shafts alone, which will have to be bought in, can be more than the price of a basic commercially manufactured model. However, the main attraction of building a vehicle at home is to be able to produce a style or design that cannot be bought and, in such cases, relative costs are of lesser importance. It is advisable to copy the main specifications from another vehicle to ensure correct proportions and basic measurements, then personal preference can select the shape and style of the body. Particular attention should be paid to the height of the seat and the amount of legroom available, the ease of access, and the balance of the vehicle if it is a two-wheeler. A sliding or adjustable seat is the easiest way of ensuring correct balance. The framework of the body needs to be extremely strong because of the severe stress it will be subjected to from different angles, and the suspension needs to be adequate for the weight of the body and the purpose for which the vehicle will be used. The design of the body may dictate the type of springs and whether the shafts are cab-style or full-length and fitted inside or outside the body. The actual body

panels can be solid wood, wooden slats, plywood, sheet metal or even basketwork, but the likely overall weight of the vehicle should be borne in mind when choosing materials to ensure that the weight and size of the vehicle are compatible.

In recent years, a number of vehicle manufacturers have started supplying vehicles in kit form, which can be assembled at home, and in many cases, it is possible to purchase optional extras or to modify the basic design with a little imagination and careful work to produce a more distinctive or specialised model. It is also possible to buy basic manufactured vehicles in undercoat only, which are then ready to paint and finish off at home.

## SUMMARY

***When choosing a vehicle make sure:***
- It is suitable for the purpose intended
- It is sound and roadworthy
- It will fit the horse

***Essential measurements to fit vehicle to horse:***
- Length of shaft from tip to front of vehicle
- Width of shafts at tug stops and breeching dees
- Distance from ground to tug stop when the floor of the vehicle is level

# 4

# DRIVING HARNESS

## Parts of the Harness

A set of single private driving harness **(Figs. 10**, **11)** is made up of at least 36 parts, which together comprise the means by which the horse is attached to the vehicle. Apart from the wide range of materials that can be used in the manufacture of harness, the actual styles can also vary to an extent according to the type and weight of the vehicle, the size and build of the horse, and the sort of driving for which the harness is required. As every set of harness must include a number of essential parts, there is limited scope for variation in the design, which has altered very little over the last two hundred years.

### Bridle

The function of the bridle is to support the bit in the horse's mouth and provide the means of controlling the horse through the reins. A driving bridle differs from a riding bridle in a number of respects, notably that the former has blinkers, which are sewn onto the cheekpieces and which serve several purposes, to prevent the horse seeing the moving wheels of the vehicle behind (which may frighten him) and to prevent the leader reins from catching the eyes of the wheel horse(s) in a team or tandem. They also prevent the horse's attention being distracted by things alongside or behind him and also serve the purpose of protecting the horse's eyes from the whip. Blinkers, also known as winkers or blinds, can be square, dee-shaped, round or hatchet-shaped **(Fig. 12)** to suit personal preferences, and should have sufficient convex curve so that they fit snugly against the horse's face without risk of pressing on the eyes or impeding the horse's forward vision **(20)**.

*Fig. 12* Types of blinker – clockwise from top left, square, round, dee and hatchet

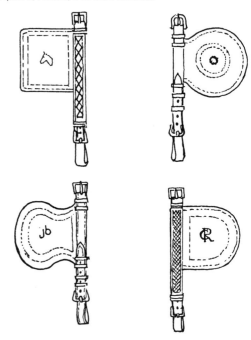

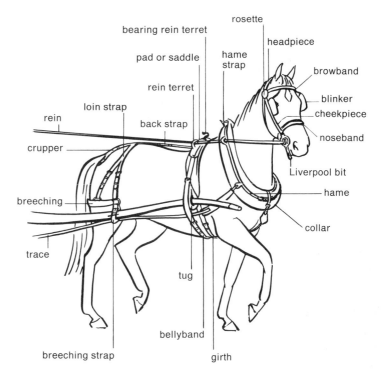

*Fig. 10* Single harness
with full collar
*Fig. 11* (*Below*) Single
harness (rear view)

rosette
bearing rein terret
pad or saddle
hame strap
headpiece
browband
blinker
rein terret
cheekpiece
loin strap
noseband
rein
back strap
crupper
Liverpool bit
hame
breeching
collar
trace
tug
bellyband
breeching strap
girth

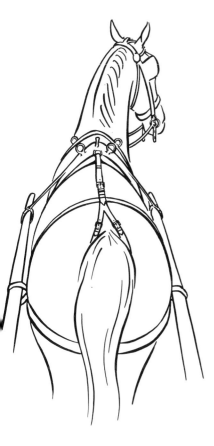

**20** As well as half-cup blinkers
in which some horses go better
than conventional blinkers, this
pony, harnessed for a cross
country marathon, is wearing a
cavesson noseband with a flash
noseband attached to prevent
him evading the bit by opening
his mouth, and a nylon
headcollar for emergencies

The cheekpieces have a buckle and billet at the lower end for the bit, and a buckle at the top for attachment to the front pair of billets on the crownpiece. The rear pair of billets are for the throat-latch, which is a short strap with buckles at either end; its purpose is to help prevent the bridle slipping off over the horse's ears. A small buckle in the centre of the crownpiece takes the winkerstay or blinker adjustment strap, which slips through a loop sewn onto the back of the browband before dividing and being sewn to the upper front of each blinker. By shortening or lengthening this strap the blinkers can be drawn closer or widened as required. The central crownpiece buckle also takes the face-piece or face-drop, a decorative piece of leather buckled under the winkerstay and passing through the browband loop. Some crownpieces have dee-rings or a third billet sewn onto each side of the crownpiece to take a bearing rein. The browband may be plain or decorated with a facing of continuous metal squares or links, and at each end there is usually a circular metal rosette, which has a bracket on the back through which the end loops of the browband pass. The cheekpiece and throat-latch billets of the crownpiece slip through the browband loop on either side of the rosette bracket and prevent the rosette moving. The noseband keeps the cheekpieces and blinkers close to the sides of the horse's head so that he cannot see behind, and to do this the billets of the cheekpieces pass through an inner loop on the sides of the noseband, around the bit rings, back through the outer loops on the noseband and onto the buckle. This is far more effective than a noseband on a separate supporting strap. An adjustment buckle on the back of the noseband under the horse's jaw should enable the noseband to be tightened to prevent the horse evading the bit by opening his mouth.

## Bearing reins

Bearing reins are rarely fitted on English harness now, although in America they are still standard on many types of harness. Their purpose is artificially to improve a horse's head carriage but they can also be helpful in restraining difficult or unruly horses. There are two types of bearing reins, those that operate on a pulley and those that are attached direct. Both types use a bridoon snaffle which goes in the horse's mouth just above the curb bit. For the pulley system, a special roller is attached to the bridoon and the bearing rein, which is buckled to the third billet on the crownpiece, passes down through the rollers on the bit then up through the rings, which are fixed to short leather straps called bridoon hangers attached to the dees on the sides of the crownpiece. Alternatively, they may thread through metal loops near the buckles on the throat-latch before terminating in two metal rings, although some bearing reins join to form one continuous strap behind the horse's neck. A flat leather strap with a buckle for adjustment connects the ends of the bearing rein to the hook in the centre of the driving pad. The direct type of bearing rein simply clips onto the bridoon bit before passing through the bridoon hanger rings or throat-latch loops and back via an adjustable strap to the hook in the pad. To ease slipping through the pulleys and rings, most bearing reins are either rolled leather or cord.

## Driving bits

Driving bits come in an almost infinite variety, each designed to produce a different action or serve a particular function. The most widely used is the Liverpool bit **(Fig. 13)**, which can be made with fixed or swivel cheeks and a variety of mouthpieces. Some have mouthpieces that slide

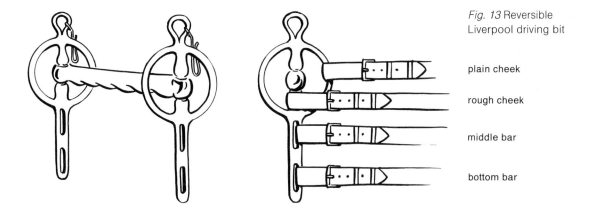

Fig. 13 Reversible
Liverpool driving bit

plain cheek

rough cheek

middle bar

bottom bar

up and down on swivel cheeks, and others have longer cheeks to increase the leverage potential and therefore the severity of the bit. The reins can be attached to the bit in a number of positions to vary the action. In plain cheek position there is no curb action, which makes this the mildest option while rough cheek position produces slight influence of the curb. Middle bar position is more severe because of the leverage obtained, and bottom bar is extremely severe and is rarely used. By using a standard curb chain enclosed in a rubber sheath, or a leather curb strap, the action is milder whereas shortening the chain on the bit hooks increases the severity. The curb chain should always be twisted until it lies flat as an uneven chain can cause the horse nearly as much discomfort as one which is unduly tight. Most horses go kindly in a Liverpool bit with a plain mouthpiece and sliding swivel cheeks, and with the reins buckled onto plain or rough cheek position, although it is worth finding out what the horse is used to in order to avoid unnecessary changes.

The double ring or Wilson snaffle (**Fig. 14**) is a useful bit especially for horses which dislike a curb and, although it is not so smart as a Liverpool driving bit for the showring, it is excellent for most other types of driving. The cheekpieces of the

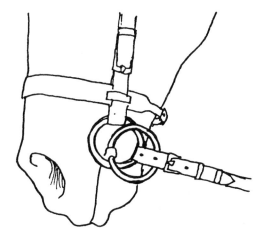

Fig. 14 Wilson or double-ring snaffle – correct method of attaching reins and cheekpieces

bridle should be attached to the floating reins and the reins either buckled around both the fixed and floating rings for a mild action or around just the fixed rings for a very severe action. The jointed mouthpiece is usually plain but twisted examples are available, again increasing the severity.

The elbow bit is very similar to the Liverpool driving bit in its action and is also produced with fixed or swivel cheeks and a variety of mouthpieces, including one which is plain on one side and rough on the other so that the reversible swivel cheeks enable it to be used either way. Many Liverpool driving bits also have this facility, the curb chain hooks being flipped over to the appropriate side. The special feature of an elbow bit is the cheeks, which are set back at an angle to prevent the horse taking hold of them in his teeth, but the selection of rein positions offer the same choice of severity as a Liverpool driving bit.

The Buxton bit **(Fig. 15)** is an ornate-looking curb bit with elegantly-curved cheeks joined by a crossbar at the bottom, and it is generally reserved for very formal turnouts. Its action is similar to a Liverpool driving bit and it is produced with the same variety of mouthpieces and fixed or swivel cheeks. Buxton bits are more likely to be used with pairs or teams than singles.

The bit should be of adequate width for the horse's mouth as too narrow a bit or one that is worn where the swivel cheeks pass through the ends of the mouthpiece can pinch the corners of the horse's mouth. A bit with a thick, smooth mouth-

piece should be selected as a thin mouthpiece increases the severity of the bit and, for preference, it should be stainless steel, although solid nickel bits are perfectly serviceable. In recent years large quantities of cheap, plated bits have been imported from the Far East but these should be avoided as the poor quality metal is prone to bend or break and the thin plating flakes off in time leaving a rough surface, which can give the horse a sore mouth.

## Collars

There are two types of collar, the full or neck collar **(Fig. 16)**, and the breast or Dutch collar **(Fig. 17)**. Although a full collar is preferable as it distributes the draught weight of the vehicle more evenly over the shoulders, a breast collar has certain advantages. Firstly, it is easier to fit as it can be adjusted to suit horses of varying height and type, whereas a full collar has to be fitted with care to ensure that it neither rocks on the shoulders, which would cause soreness, nor presses on the windpipe. A full collar that fits a horse at the beginning of the season may be too small when the animal is fitter and muscled up a couple of months later, so two or more full collars of different sizes are usually needed, which can be expensive. Making full collars is a highly-skilled job, hence their high price, but breast collars, which are easier to make, are much cheaper to buy and only one is generally needed. A breast collar **(25)** is also lighter in weight but more liable to cause collar sores because the weight of the vehicle is concentrated over a smaller area of the shoulders. Basically, breast collars are fine for light work but a full collar is preferable if heavier work is being undertaken, especially in a hilly area or on soft going like muddy tracks. If a breast collar is chosen, select one that is

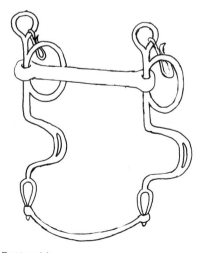

*Fig. 15* Buxton bit

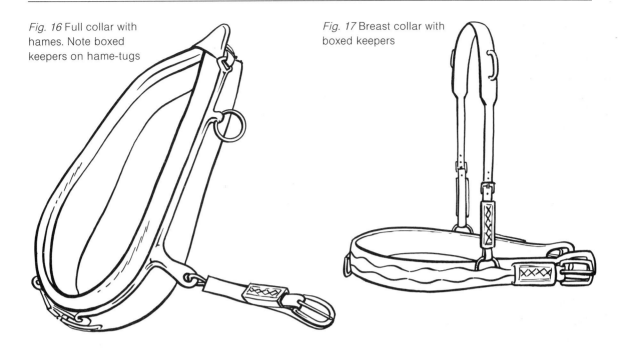

*Fig. 16* Full collar with
hames. Note boxed
keepers on hame-tugs

*Fig. 17* Breast collar with
boxed keepers

not too narrow and is adequately padded
on the inside. A neck strap with buckles at
the sides for adjustment supports the
breast collar, which usually will have
buckles at either end for the traces. Some
types of breast collar have traces sewn to
their ends, in which case chain links at the
ends of the traces or short leather extensions with buckles enable the length of the
traces to be altered. If a breast collar is
used, the vehicle must have a swingletree
to avoid rubbing the horse's shoulders as
the collar slides from side to side with each
stride.

Full collars come in a variety of designs.
Open-topped collars have a buckle and
short strap to connect the upper points so
that the collar can be put on the horse
without slipping it over his head if he is
headshy. Piped collars have a depression
in the middle of the lower part to ensure
that they cannot press on the horse's
windpipe, which could make him jib or
might even affect his wind in time, and
Princes Forewale or Kay collars have the
lining brought around to the front of the
forewale, which looks neater. Collars can

also be straight or curved back in a lazy S
shape and tapered at the top. Some people
believe that a straight collar is less likely
to rub than a curved collar, which looks
more stylish and is therefore more
favoured for the showring especially as a
curved collar shows off the horse's front
and gives the optical illusion of the horse
having a better length of rein than may
actually be the case.

## Hames

The hames, which are usually made of
steel plated with brass or nickel, lie in the
groove between the forewale and after-
wale and are secured in place by leather
hame straps at the top and bottom. A fixed
or swivelling rein terret is attached a little
way from the top of each hame, and about
a third of the way up from the bottom there
is a metal spur called the draught pull to
which the traces are attached either directly by being sewn onto an open ring or
indirectly via a hame tug, which is rivet-
ted to a metal clip fixed to the hame. The
hame tug has a buckle to which the trace is

attached allowing alterations to the length of the trace to be made, and a slot called the crew or dart hole at the other end of the trace slips over the trace hook on the swingletree or on the vehicle itself. Chain trace ends or short leather couplings permit trace length adjustments when the traces are sewn onto the hames. It is very important that the hames fit snugly onto the collar as badly fitting hames could slip off the collar with disastrous results. It is much easier to get hames to fit a straight collar than a curved collar, as with the latter the hames must follow the double curve shape of the collar or when the hamestraps are tightened the hames will pull the collar out of shape.

## False martingales

Many sets of harness have a false martingale, which buckles around the bottom of the collar including the hames at one end and has a loop through which the girth passes at the other. An adjustment buckle enables it to be lengthened or shortened as necessary. Apart from being decorative, a false martingale keeps the bottom of the collar down although those that buckle to a dee on the middle underside of a breast collar are really just cosmetic and not functional.

## Driving pad or saddle

The pad or saddle should be of sufficient width to be in keeping with the style and weight of the vehicle. A narrow pad with curved or swell panels may look fine with an elegant gig but out of place with a more utilitarian and heavier country cart for

which a broader pad with straight panels may be more appropriate. It should be adequately stuffed on the underside to stand it well clear of the horse's spine, and it should be possible to see daylight through the gullet at all times even when it is girthed up. For driving a single horse to a two-wheeled vehicle, the backband should be of the running type which passes through a channel in the saddle itself so that it can slide backwards and forwards. Fixed backbands, sewn under the skirt of the saddle are better when driving a four-wheeler with shafts that can be moved independently as, if a running backband is used, one shaft can drop down while the other is consequently raised. The shaft

21   A Morgan horse driven to a road cart. The leather footwell is intended to protect the driver from dirt thrown up by the horse's hoofs. Note the wraparound bellyband used on some types of American harness

tugs, which are buckled to the backband, support the shafts and they can either be of the open type, which is a fixed leather loop, or of the French or Tilbury pattern, which fasten tightly around the shaft **(Fig. 18) (23)**. Open tugs are used with nearly all two-wheelers so that when the vehicle is balanced the shafts ride freely in the tugs and do not transmit the trotting motion of the horse to the vehicle. For this reason the bellyband, which has a buckle at either end to attach to the ends of the backband to form a continuous loop, should be loose enough to allow the tugs some play. On some harness there is a loop on the girth through which the bellyband passes to keep it in place. A few two-

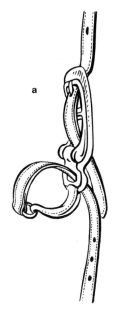

*Fig. 18* a French or Tilbury tug b open tug

wheeled vehicles, including Tilbury gigs and those with shafts of exaggerated curve, and most four-wheelers ride better when French or Tilbury tugs are used.

On either side of the pad saddle are the terrets, which screw into the tree and through which the reins pass. On webbing harness or less expensive leather sets, the rein terrets are often just metal rings sewn onto the pad by means of a webbing or leather tab, and sometimes the terret is merely a webbing or leather loop, which is not very satisfactory as the reins do not slide through them freely. Between the terrets on all but the cheaper sets of harness is the bearing rein hook, and at the back of the saddle is a dee-ring onto which the backstrap is buckled. The crupper is either sewn or buckled to the

22   Breeching straps can be wrapped around the shaft before buckling. The trace bearer is to support the trace without impeding its direct line of draught from the collar via the swingletree to the axle

backstrap and its purpose is to prevent the pad slipping forward onto the horse's withers. On good quality leather harness, the crupper is stuffed with linseed but on cheaper leather or webbing harness the crupper may be just a loop of soft folded leather and it is important to ensure that this is very supple and cannot rub the horse's dock.

## Breeching

The breeching comprises a long broad strap which is supported by a loin or quarter strap which passes through a loop on the backstrap. It is attached to the breeching dees on the shafts by breeching straps and it prevents the vehicle running forward onto the horse, especially when going downhill **(22)**. Full breeching, as it is known, has the added advantage of also doubling as a kicking strap. On some harness, long breeching is used which has

*Fig. 19* False or Brown's
patent breeching

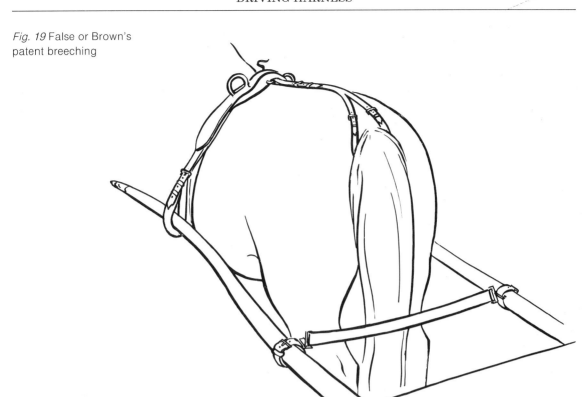

**Reins**

The reins can vary in width according to personal preference although very wide reins can be cumbersome while very narrow reins can prove difficult to hold in wet weather or if the horse is pulling. Some reins have plaited, laced or folded and sewn handparts to make them easier to grip, and others have a strip of leather laid and stitched down the centre and are known as Melton or 'flat and laid on' reins. The reins must suit the type of turnout as reins that are too short can be snatched from the hand if the horse stumbles, but if too long they can be a nuisance and get caught up in the driver's feet. The reins required for driving a single horse to a park phaeton will need to be much longer than those for driving the same animal to a gig because of the distance between the horse's head and the driving seat.

lengthened breeching straps which buckle onto the tugs. This style of breeching is thought by some to be tidier in appearance and it also causes less scratching to the paintwork on the shafts although a band of protective leather sewn tightly around the shaft where the breeching dee is screwed on will protect the paintwork from being marked. Similarly, a leather sleeve extending from the shaft tip to behind the tug stop will prevent the paintwork on the end of the shaft being marked as a result of sliding it through the tug. Although not actually part of a set of harness, 'false' breeching consists of a broad leather strap, which is buckled across the shafts about 20cm (8in) from the dashboard by means of metal dees on the shafts, and this strap presses against the horse's quarters on a downhill and enables him to hold the vehicle back **(fig. 19)**.

## Types of Harness

### Private driving or gig harness

Private driving or 'gig' harness, as it is also misleadingly known, can be made with either plain keepers or boxed keepers on the bridle, tugs, hame tugs, backband and loinstrap. Boxed keepers are usually embossed with a decorative pattern and can look smarter especially in the showring but the choice is up to personal preference.

23    Gig harness. Mrs Bette Lambert driving a part-bred Welsh pony to a Parkgate gig. Telescopic shock absorbers have been fitted between the springs and the body of the vehicle to strengthen the suspension. Note also the Tilbury tugs on the harness

### Trade harness

Trade harness, which is designed to be used with trade or commercial vehicles and is therefore unsuitable for private driving, is more substantially made with a wider pad and fuller collar. It is also more ornate with red, yellow or other coloured leather trim, and some sets have decorative leather pieces called 'kidney or rib beaters' hanging down on either side of the backband. White metal furnishings are usual, and the buckles are frequently in the shape of horse-shoes hence its name 'horse-shoe buckle trade harness.'

### Vanner harness

Heavier but plainer harness with the minimum amount of white metal fittings is known as vanner harness after the vanner

*Fig. 20* Pair harness with breast collars and trace bearers. Note the Liverpool driving bits with offside horse on middle bar and nearside on rough cheek

or medium-weight draught horses for which it was designed. This type of harness, which was used with heavy commercial vehicles as shown by the broad pad and heavy duty traces, turns up frequently at second-hand harness sales and although it is strong, it is generally too heavy to be used for private driving.

## Skeleton harness

At the other extreme, very lightweight harness with a narrow pad, breast collar and no breeching is used for showing Hackneys or, in America, horses in fine harness classes. By having as little harness as possible on the horse, it does not distract attention from the animal itself, and as the driving is confined to a level showring and a very lightweight vehicle is used, it is perfectly adequate. Skeleton harness is too fine for general pleasure driving, and the same applies to the lightweight harness used for racing trotters and pacers, it is unsuited to anything other than use with a light sulky on a smooth level track.

## Pair harness

Pair harness **(Fig. 20) (24)** is similar in many respects to two sets of single harness, the main differences being that the collars have a ring or link at the front to take the pole straps, which attach to the pole end, and the hame tugs are longer and buckle on to the tug straps on the pad, with the bellyband fastened to the two short leather straps which hang down at either side from the tug buckles. The trace ends have loops to fasten to the roller bolts on the splinter bar of the vehicle, and breeching is usually used only for driving in hilly country or if the vehicle has no brake. The reins are made with couplings so that the nearside rein controls the nearside of each horse, and vice versa.

## Materials used in harness manufacture

Although harness was always traditionally made of leather, in recent years new types of material have been used for harness making in an attempt to reduce manufacturing costs while still maintain-

ing the strength and durability of the product. Ease of maintenance and extremely light weight are additional benefits claimed for harness made from some of these modern materials, although their disadvantages sometimes outweigh their beneficial qualities and, from both an economical and practical point of view, they may prove to be less suitable than leather harness in the long run.

Webbing harness is now extensively used for competitive driving as it is strong and light and requires little maintenance as it can be placed in an old pillow case and put through a domestic washing machine to clean it. Provided that the webbing is thick, soft and adequately padded under

24 Mr Jack Stamper driving his chestnut geldings, Tom and Jerry, to a Stanhope phaeton. Pole chains are sometimes used instead of straps with a Stanhope phaeton to give it more of a road coach flavour

the pad and breast collar, it is serviceable and roughly half the cost of leather harness. On some cheaper sets, the metal eyelets through which the tongues of the buckles pass may loosen or even come out, causing holes to tear or fray, and also the webbing can become limp and stretch which can cause the harness to fit badly or become difficult to adjust evenly. Nylon or plastic-coated webbing can tend to rub the horse especially if he is sweated up as it absorbs little moisture, although a percentage of nylon in cotton webbing is quite usual. As full collars cannot successfully be made from any material other than leather stuffed with straw (although metal, straw and even inflatable rubber collars were experimented with at one time and sometimes used on horses with sore shoulders) webbing harness always has a breast collar. Using a full collar with webbing harness is obviously an option but makes the set unmatched and only emphasises the fact that webbing harness never looks as smart as leather harness. An additional point is that the pad on a webbing set is rarely built on a tree and is therefore neither so strong nor so rigid and supportive as a proper pad, and it is important to ensure that there is sufficient padding under the pad to lift it well clear of the horse's spine. Buffalo hide is strong and less likely to rub than nylon webbing, and those sets that are a combination of webbing faced with leather are often excellent as they can successfully unite the advantages of both materials. Car seat belting is sometimes used for traces for combined driving or other types of driving where the harness will be subjected to extreme strain and, despite its untraditional appearance, it is very strong, easily obtainable and cheap.

## Colour

The custom with leather harness was to use black harness for town driving to a painted vehicle, and brown harness for country driving to a varnished vehicle although these traditions are no longer observed except perhaps in the showring. The reins should always be brown even with black harness as the dye might otherwise come off onto the driver's hands or clothes. Some sets of show harness have the blinkers, collar and pad faced with patent leather, which is japanned to give it a very glossy surface. This looks very smart but it scratches easily and can soon become shabby unless looked after very carefully. As such, patent leather harness is not really suited to everyday use, whereas plain leather harness will polish up again and again and retain its smartness.

## Metal fittings

The metal fittings on the harness should match the fittings on the vehicle, and should be brass for preference although nickel is also acceptable. Manganese bronze, an alloy similar in appearance to brass, can also be used but some other alloys used on cheap harness are prone to bend or even break and should be avoided. Steel tongues in all the harness buckles will help ensure that the buckles are strong enough for their purpose. A discreet monogram on the blinkers, face drop, and either side of the pad is fine and can make the harness look more distinctive.

## Size and fit

Harness is generally described as either full-size, cob-size or pony-size, which can be very misleading as the build and conformation rather than the height of a horse or pony can dictate the size of harness required **(Fig. 21)**. A cob-size set of harness may well fit both a pony of draught type and a big horse of light build with a fine quality head, so it is essential to take basic measurements of the horse against which to check the size of likely sets of harness if buying at sales. Bridle and girth measurements should pose no problems but full collar sizes are more complicated as there is no accurate method of measuring a horse to ascertain what size of collar he will need. If possible, try a few borrowed collars on him until one which fits well is found then use the measurements of this collar as a rough guide when looking at collars in sales. If a full collar is too long it will slip upwards and back when the horse is in draught, but too short a collar will press on the windpipe, making it difficult for the animal to work. A collar that is too narrow will pinch the horse's neck and possibly cause galls, whereas

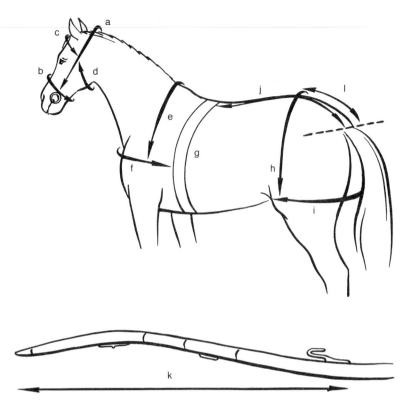

*Fig. 21* Measurements for harness from a maker or supplier **a** head, corner of mouth to corner of mouth over poll **b** nose, just above the top of the bit **c** brow, to back of headstall strap **d** throat, rear of jawbone under ear **e** over withers, collar line to collar line **f** chest, rear of elbow muscle to same **g** girth, all round **h** over croup, breeching level to same **i** breeching, stifle to stifle, taut **j** back length, rear of pad to top of tail **k** shaft length of vehicle (shaft tip to trace hook) **l** croup to tail **m** shape of back: make a template with coathanger, electric cable or similar, mould it to shape where pad will lie (be firm!), draw inside shape onto paper without distorting and send paper with other measurements

one that is too wide will rock from side to side and the friction will cause soreness and eventually collar galls. The collar should lie evenly against the shoulders and should move as little as possible when the horse is in draught; there should be sufficient room to slip a hand between the lower part of the collar and the horse's windpipe at all times. A false martingale can help to keep a collar from riding up and tipping provided that the collar fits well otherwise, and it is essential to check that a collar that fits when the horse is out of draught still fits when he is actually pulling. It could be that the draught pulls on the hames are too low, causing the collar to tip forward and friction to occur under the point of draught. Choosing a set of harness with a breast collar avoids the problems and difficulties of finding a full collar and hames that fit properly.

If buying harness privately, ask to try it on the horse first to make sure it fits and that there is adequate scope for adjustment if he puts weight on or slims down during the season. Ideally, there should always be at least one adjustment hole either side of the one accommodating the buckle tongue on every strap on the harness. A girth that is too short can be remedied by using a girth extension, and traces can have extension straps added or be replaced, but other parts of the harness that do not fit are more difficult and expensive to alter or replace and may render the whole set unsuitable.

## Soundness

Apart from fitting correctly, the other essential factor is that harness should be sound. Many people new to driving buy old harness as it is cheaper than new and may look reasonably smart and strong. Often it has hung for years in a barn or outhouse and the leather is so dried out it will break as soon as it is put under any strain unless thoroughly cleaned and oiled, and even this is not guaranteed to make it safe. Check old harness meticulously for cracked or perished leather, rotted stitching and corroded buckle tongues, particularly those parts which take the most strain, like the hame tugs, hame straps and traces. The billets that fasten around the bit are especially prone to rot due to being in contact with the horse's saliva, and the girth can often become brittle and crack because of the salt in the horse's sweat. Check all the billets for wear, see that the metal furnishings match, and make sure the pad tree is not broken, by examining it for any looseness or movement in the arch. A saddler's bill for repairing defective parts and renewing stitching can soon make a cheap set of old harness very expensive.

*Fig. 22* Carriage or trap lamps **a** oval-fronted, **b** square-fronted, **c** rear lamp

## *Driving Accoutrements*

### Carriage Lamps

Carriage or trap lamps **(Fig. 22)** are now used only for decorative purposes as the light they give out is too weak to illuminate a vehicle sufficiently to make driving after dark safe and, in view of the number of cars on the roads and the speed at which they travel in relation to a horse, a slow-moving and poorly-lit horse-drawn vehicle would put itself at great risk. Even so, lamps complete the correct appointments on a vehicle and are mandatory in all but a few specialized classes in the showring. They come in a wide variety of sizes and types, from enormous ornate examples for formal carriages to simple, functional lamps for humbler turnouts **(Fig. 22)**.

The body of the lamp is invariably square with the front and outer side panels of bevelled glass, and the other two sides of pressed metal lined, like the base, with

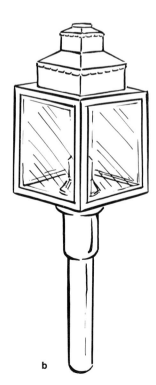
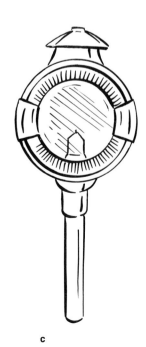

a                  b                c

reflectors of silver plated copper which throw the light sideways onto the road and forwards towards the horse. The rear panel often has a small circular red glass pane in the centre to act as a rear light. The front of the lamp can be square, round, oval or fluted, and some have a deep brass or white metal rim on the front with matching stem and bands, and others are merely edged with a narrow polished metal trim. The tops vary from oval or round fluted examples to more stylish types with two or three square caps of diminishing size, which are known as pagoda tops. The lamp is fuelled by a candle housed in a metal tube fixed to the base of the lamp to form the stem. Only the tip of the candle and the wick show through the base of the lamp body where they are kept in place by a circular metal fitting. A spring in the bottom of the stem under the candle expands slowly as the candle burns down to press the candle head continually against the fitting. The candle can be renewed when necessary by opening the hinged back panel of the lamp and pulling a small lever, which releases the catch securing the stem, which slides down and out. On some lamps, the stems are secured by a simple screw thread. Lamps fuelled by kerosene, carbide or even gas were manufactured in the last century but examples of these are now rare and too valuable for general use.

The lamps must be in keeping with the vehicle and of a suitable size. Square lamps usually look better on vehicles of a more angular design like dogcarts, and oval-fronted lamps are more suited to vehicles with more elegant lines like gigs. Large ornate lamps with engraved glass panels, trade lamps with horseshoe fronts, or massive round-faced commercial vehicle lamps are all unsuitable for a private driving vehicle. A rear lamp, which is like a half-size edition of an ordinary lamp but with a single red glass in the front, can be carried on the back of the vehicle by means of a special angled bracket.

## Driving Whips

A driving whip must be carried at all times as it may be necessary to use it to reinforce verbal commands with a lazy horse, to correct a fault, or to give signals to other road users. There are three main types of driving whip but of these, the buggy whip, which is a straight tapered switch of about 150 cm (5 ft) and made of steel-lined cane or fibre-glass, is suitable only for race driving or for certain types of American show classes. The drop thong whip has the leather thong attached to the straight cane stick by a small leather loop at the end, and the English bow top whip has a stock made of a pliable material like holly, hickory, blackthorn, cane or whalebone to which is bound the tapering thong of plaited leather using a goose-quill to give the whip its distinctive bow top shape. A short, coloured, silk lash is attached to the end of the thong of both types of whip. Bow top whips with fibre-glass stocks covered in plaited thread are now available; they are very good and much cheaper than traditional holly whips. Both drop thong and bow top whips usually have a leather-covered or plaited leather handpart between the metal cap at the end and the collar or metal ferrule **(Fig. 23)**. As a rough guide the stock of a whip should range from about 110 cm (3 ft 6 in) for a small pony, to 120 cm (4 ft) for a larger pony or cob, and up to 150 cm (5 ft) for a big horse, with a thong of about 120 cm (4 ft) in all cases.

When buying a whip, it is important to choose one that balances well in the hand. In good whips, the butt-cap is weighted with lead and the handpart is often lined in steel to counterbalance the weight of the rest of the stock and the thong so that

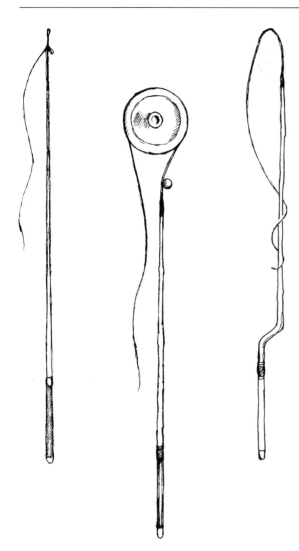

the whip is not heavy to hold and does not cause the wrist to ache. Private driving whips should have the minimum amount of embellishment in terms of ornate handles or additional ferrules up the stock, which would be more appropriate to a trade turnout. Second-hand whips should be checked over for breaks or damage to the stock, often caused by carelessly leaving the whip on the ground and the horse standing on it, and for damage to the goose-quill in bow tops causing the thong to hang limply from the stock. Whips with ivory handles, hall-marked silver mounts, or engraved metal collars are always in greater demand than other whips and will be correspondingly more expensive.

## Driving aprons

A knee rug or apron **(Fig. 24)** should always be worn when driving as it keeps the wearer clean, dry and warm. For summer driving, a lightweight linen apron in a discreet colour or a blue and white 'tattersall' check will prevent horsehair, dust from the road, or oil from the reins marking the clothes, but in winter weather an apron of heavier material like Bedford cord will be warmer. For wet

*Fig. 23* Driving whips – from left: drop-thong whip, bow-top whip on reel, dog-leg whip

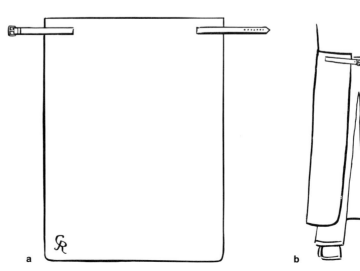

*Fig. 24* **a** Driving apron with monogram, **b**

a

b

weather driving, a waterproof apron of waxed or rubberized cotton lined in checked material or wool is best. Beige material, called 'drab' in years gone by, blends well with most colours and does not show the dirt and horsehair as noticeably as a dark colour would, but navy, dark green or maroon aprons to match the paintwork of the vehicle are quite acceptable. Bright colours, bold checks or patterned fabrics are wrong for a driving apron. A single apron should be long enough to reach to the wearer's ankles, and wide enough to meet at the back where it is fastened with a small buckle. As an apron can be an impediment if the driver needs to get out of the vehicle quickly, some people either do not fasten the buckle or have an apron without a buckle which just tucks in under the wearer when he or she sits down. Alternatively, strips of 'velcro' can be used to fasten the apron. The hem may be sewn with three or four rows of stitching or bound with material of a similar or complementary colour. Double aprons cover the legs of both the driver and passenger and have a ring sewn into the centre of the apron a little way from the top edge with a short leather strap, which buckles to the middle of the rail behind the seat. This keeps the apron in place and prevents it slipping down onto the floor. The driver and passenger then fold the outer sides over themselves when they get into the vehicle and tuck the edge in when they sit down.

## SUMMARY

*When buying a set of harness, check that:*
- It is suitable for its purpose
- It will fit the horse (especially the collar)
- It is sound and serviceable

# *Part 2*
# SETTING OFF

# 5

# THE PRINCIPLES OF DRIVING

## *Correct Harnessing Procedure*

When harnessing a horse prior to 'putting to,' the same sequence of stages should always be followed **(Fig. 25)**, as careless mistakes are less likely to be made when the same familiar routine is practised, and also the horse will get used to the consistent format and will feel more confident with it. Only one person should do the actual harnessing while an assistant holds the horse but watches for any errors like a rein not slipped through a terret, which may have been missed by the person putting the harness on the horse. The work should be done methodically and conscientiously but not hurried, with all billets secured in their keepers and everything checked as it is put on.

The horse is usually held by means of a headcollar and lead rein while the harness is brought and either hung up or laid out on the ground in such a way that each part is easily accessible in the order required. If the harness is being laid out on the ground, an old horserug or blanket will help to keep it clean and prevent scratching any parts faced with patent leather. It needs to be within easy reach but not so close that the horse could inadvertently stand on it or where it could get tangled around the assistant's feet.

## Fitting the collar

The collar is always put on first, and a neck collar should be stretched to help it slip over the head by removing the hames and stretching it sideways over one knee. This temporarily widens it. The collar is then held upside down with the widest part to the top to correspond with the widest part of the horse's head and slipped very carefully over the head. A horse's eyes and ears are very sensitive and force must never be used to get a tight collar on as this is likely to make the horse headshy and difficult to harness in future. While the collar is still upside down and at the top of the neck, the hames connected by the bottom hame strap and with the traces attached but coiled around themselves are placed in position in the groove in the collar. The top hame strap, now at the bottom as the collar is still upside down, is fastened to secure the hames in place while the collar is turned the right way up.

*Fig. 25* Harnessing procedure **a** stretch collar, **b** put on collar upside down, **c** attach hames, **d** turn collar (in the direction the mane lies) and tidy mane, **e** place pad and loosely fasten girth, **f** put on crupper, ensuring no tail hairs are caught, **g** place pad forward in correct position and fasten girth, **h** put on bridle, **i** fasten buckles and curb chain – note chain twisted until flat, **j** attach reins

This should be done at the narrowest part of the horse's throat and with the direction of the mane to make it easier to turn, and the collar can then be pushed down until it lies in position against the shoulders. The top hame strap can now be tightened so that there is no danger of the hames working loose. The hame straps should be put on the collar with the buckle on the offside hame as it is easier to tighten the hame straps by pulling the billet towards you rather than away. A properly fitting collar should lie evenly on the shoulders with enough room at the sides to slip two fingers under **(Fig. 26)**, and space enough at the front for the whole hand between the horse's windpipe and the bottom of the collar. When in draught, the full length of the collar should remain in contact with the shoulders, and there should be no tendency for the collar to tilt or rock backwards and forwards. Some slight adjustment to the collar shape can be made by tightening one hame strap and slackening the other, or vice versa, so that the hames narrow one end of the collar by pressing in on each other. Although many people put the collar on the horse with the hames attached, there is the danger of the hame tugs and traces getting in the way or even catching the horse's face, and it is impossible to widen a collar by stretching it over one knee if the hames are buckled on. If a false martingale is used, it should be buckled around the bottom of the collar and hames at this stage before the pad is put on. If the harness has a breast collar, the neckstrap should be unbuckled on the nearside to put the collar on rather than slip the collar over the horse's head. The neckstrap should then be adjusted so that the collar lies above the points of the shoulders to avoid chafing them, but below the windpipe. A false martingale on a breastcollar is buckled to the small dee in the centre of the bottom edge of the collar. The traces can either be left attached to the breastcollar or buckled on once the collar is in place but coiled around themselves in both cases. A soft sheepskin sleeve is sometimes slipped over a breast collar to make it more comfortable and less likely to rub a thin-skinned horse.

## The pad, crupper and breeching

The pad, complete with backband, tugs, bellyband, crupper, loinstrap and breeching, is put on next in one piece by placing the pad a little to the rear of the middle of the horse's back and positioning the breeching over the quarters so that it lies against the buttocks. Fastening the girth very loosely will prevent the pad falling to the ground and possibly being stood on and damaged should the horse move. Working always from the nearside, the tail is slipped through the crupper by raising it with the right hand and folding it in half then placing the crupper over the tail and easing the crupper up to the top of the dock. It is very important to make sure that no hair is caught under the crupper as this can irritate or even rub the sensitive skin on the underside of the dock, and it is essential to ensure that the crupper is well oiled and very supple. Some cruppers have buckles on the actual tailpiece in which case the nearside buckle can be undone, the tail lifted, and the crupper slipped underneath and rebuckled. Many horses dislike the crupper and show it by clamping their tail down when being harnessed, and this type of crupper can make the job much easier. Once the tail is through the crupper, the pad can be lifted forward on the back so that the backstrap prevents the saddle slipping forward but is not so tight that there is continual pressure on the horse's tail. The pad should sit roughly in the middle of the horse's back, and well clear of the withers. If the pad is placed too

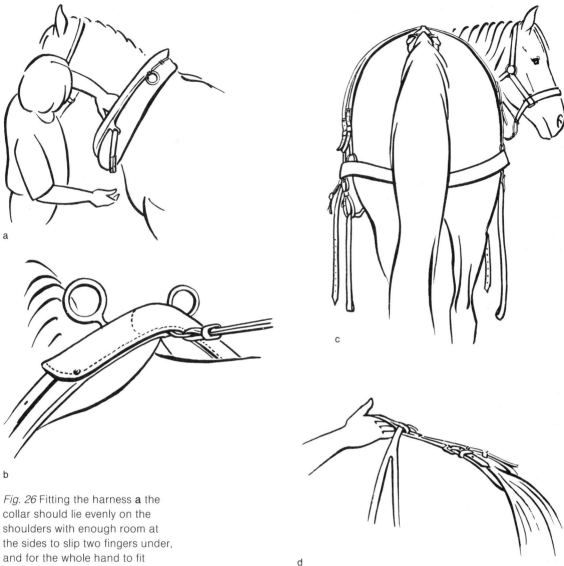

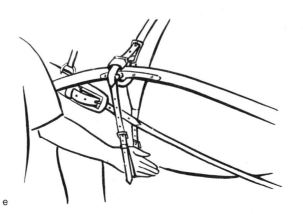

*Fig. 26* Fitting the harness **a** the collar should lie evenly on the shoulders with enough room at the sides to slip two fingers under, and for the whole hand to fit between the horse's windpipe and the bottom of the collar, **b** the pad must sit well clear of the spine, with sufficient firm padding to prevent it being drawn down onto the spine when the girth is tightened, **c** breeching – if too high the breeching can slide up under the horse's dock and if too low it can push the horse's legs from under him on a steep incline, **d** backstrap should allow a hand to be slid underneath, **e** with two-wheeled vehicles, the bellyband should permit a hand to be slipped easily between it and the girth

far forward, the girth can rub the horse's elbows or cause girth galls. As pads vary in width fittings, make sure the pad sits comfortably on the horse's back and is adequately padded on the underside. A pad which is too narrow in the tree will perch high and pinch the horse's back, and too wide a pad may bear down on the spine. Before buckling the girth, it should be passed through the loop of the false martingale if one is used. The girth on a driving pad need not be so tight as that on a riding saddle but it is as much a mistake to have a loose girth, which can rub and lead to galls, as to have an unnecessarily tight girth, which can be uncomfortable for the horse. The bellyband should be fastened loosely to prevent it swinging about and distracting the horse, especially if he has to be led to where the vehicle is parked. Some people like to buckle the breeching straps back onto themselves or even just thread the unbuckled breeching strap billets through their keepers for the same reason.

## Attaching the reins

The reins are slipped through the pad terrets and hame terrets and either left hanging down ready to buckle onto the bit or buckled temporarily to the hame terrets. The driving end is usually tucked into the offside terret or under the back-strap to keep it out of the way and to prevent the possibility of it falling onto the ground if the horse is being led to the vehicle.

## Putting on the bridle

The bridle is put on by slipping the headcollar off and buckling it loosely around the horse's neck to maintain control until the bridle is in place. The throat-latch, noseband and curb chain should all be unfastened first then, stand-ing on the nearside, the bit (including the bridoon if a bearing rein is used) is raised to the horse's mouth by the left hand while the right supports the bridle by the crown-piece. Sliding the thumb of the left hand into the side of the horse's mouth will cause him to open his mouth and the bit can be quietly slipped in taking care not to rattle the bit against his teeth, which may make him difficult to bridle in future.

The crownpiece is passed over his ears, and the forelock either left under the browband or pulled out between the winker stays but under the facedrop so there is less risk of it getting under the blinkers and obscuring his forward vision. The throat-latch should be fastened tighter than with a riding bridle but there must be enough room for the horse to flex his head without restriction from the throat-latch. There should be enough space to get two fingers under the nose-band when it is fastened, unless the horse evades the bit by opening his mouth, in which case it may need to be buckled tighter to keep his mouth shut. As with the hame straps, the buckle should be on the offside so that the billet is drawn down and outwards when tightening the noseband. The curb chain should be twisted until it lies flat then clipped onto the curb chain hook on the nearside of the bit making sure it is loose enough to allow two fingers to be comfortably slipped under it. A slack curb chain will be ineffective but a tight or twisted curb chain will hurt the horse's jaw and may cause him to jib or play-up as a result of the pain.

The fitting of the bridle is very important. The browband must be long enough so that it does not pull the crownpiece and the metal rosettes onto the base of the horse's ears, which would make him fidget or throw his head about with the inherent risk of shaking or rubbing the bridle off altogether. The blinkers can be adjusted by means of the top buckle on the cheekpieces to ensure that the centre of each blinker corresponds with the point of the eye, and the winkerstays via the centre buckle on the crownpiece should be used to alter the width of the blinkers so that they neither press on the eyes nor flap about. Blinkers which are too low may rub the top of the eye and permit the horse to see over the top of them, and loose blinkers could irritate or hurt the horse's eyes. On some cheaper harness, decorative metal motifs are sometimes attached to the blinkers and facedrop by means of metal clips which pierce the leather and are bent over on the other wide to hold them in place. These clips are very dangerous as they can injure the face or eyes and should be removed with pliers. The height of the bit in the horse's mouth is adjusted by means of the buckle and billet at the bottom of each cheekpiece so that the bit just wrinkles the corners of the mouth. The front part of the noseband must be long enough to allow the cheekpieces to hang straight, but too large a noseband would allow the cheekpieces to bulge out when pressure was put on the bit.

Finally, the reins should be buckled on to the bit, and everything given a final check before 'putting to' the vehicle. While it is important to ensure that the harness is adjusted evenly and that the traces are the same length and the tugs at the same height, counting the holes between each buckle and the end of the billet is not a fool-proof system as new harness can stretch. Also, on second-hand harness some parts, such as traces, may be replaced so that although they may appear the same they are not actually a true pair and the newer one may stretch over a period of time to gradually make the draught uneven. Regular checks when cleaning the harness should identify any problems of this type as well as any loose stitching or worn leather parts that require attention.

## Correct procedure for putting to

If the horse is harnessed up in a loosebox, care must be taken when he is led out as the blinkers will prevent him seeing on either side. The door should be opened wide and the horse slowly led out so there is no risk of him catching himself or any part of the harness on the door jamb. A horse that has been injured on a doorway or has caught the harness and frightened himself is likely to be nervous and liable to rush through doorways, and the habit is difficult to cure once established.

To put the horse to a two-wheeled vehicle (**Fig. 27**), he should be stood still and held by an assistant while the vehicle is drawn up behind him with the shafts raised well above his quarters. The traces should have been uncoiled and passed between the pad and the bellyband if open tugs are used, or outside the bellyband if Tilbury or French tugs are used, and crossed behind the pad and under the backstrap out of the way. The shafts are lowered and passed through the tugs until the tugs are up to the stops, then the traces are fastened to the tracehooks or swingle-tree making sure there are no twists in the traces, and the breeching straps are buckled around the shafts. It is quite permissible to wrap the breeching straps once or even twice around the shaft at the point of the breeching dee before buckling to achieve the correct adjustment and a tidy appearance.

Lastly, the bellyband should be tightened as necessary, remembering with a two-wheeled vehicle to leave it slack enough to allow the tugs scope to move up and down to balance the vehicle. With a four-wheeled vehicle, it is usual to stand the vehicle with its shafts in the air and bring the horse to stand in front of the vehicle so that the shafts can be lowered and put through the tugs. The procedure is then the same as for a two-wheeler except

Fig. 27 Putting the horse to the vehicle **a** the vehicle is brought to the horse, **b** the shafts are run into the tugs as far as the tugstop, **c** the traces are hooked up, **d** the breeching straps are fastened, **e** the girth is checked and tightened, **f** the horse's foreleg is drawn forward to free any wrinkled skin under the girth, **g** the bellyband is fastened

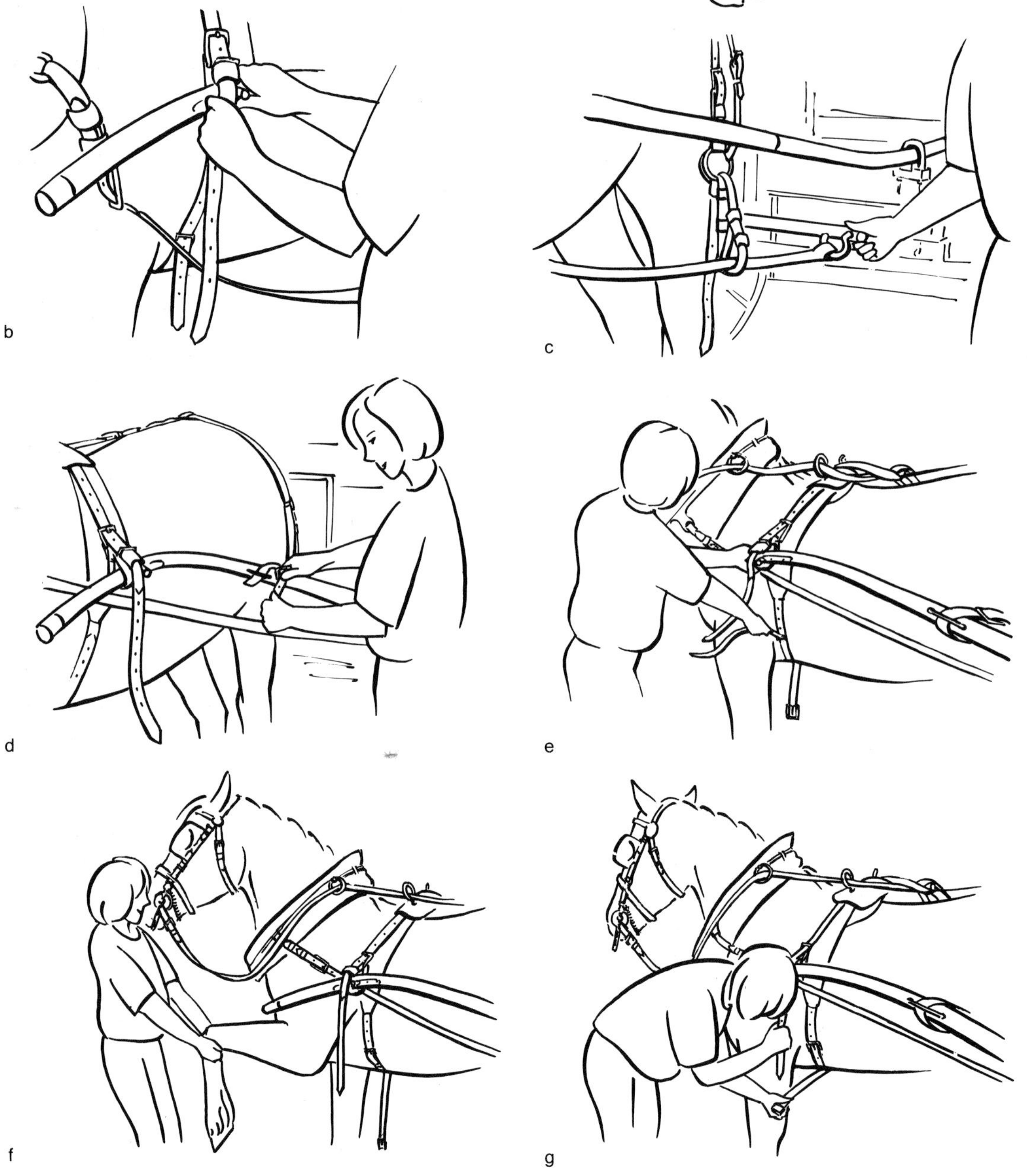

a

b

c

d

e

f

g

that the bellyband should be fastened tight to hold the shafts firmly against the pad.

The reason for having the bellyband very loose or even unfastened when putting to is that it facilitates getting the shafts through the tugs. The traces should always be hooked on before the bellyband is fastened or the breeching straps buckled so that if the horse suddenly moves, the vehicle will go with him and there is no danger of the shafts sliding out of the tugs and falling onto the ground, which may damage them.

If difficulty is experienced getting the traces to reach the trace hooks or swingletree, it is better to draw the vehicle forward a little way by pulling on the steps than to make the horse step back, as we want to teach the horse to remain absolutely stationary when being harnessed and put to. The breeching straps should always be buckled around the dees furthest from the dashboard so that the horse has full freedom of movement when trotting but the vehicle is prevented from touching the horse even on the steepest downhill. If the breeching is adjusted too low it has a tendency to push the horse's hindlegs from under him, but if too high it could ride up under his dock with disastrous results.

If false breeching is used rather than full breeching, this should be buckled onto the vehicle using the dees on the shafts nearest the dashboard, and remember to do this before the horse is brought out. The tugs should be at such a height that the floor of the vehicle is absolutely level when put to correctly, the traces should be drawn firm but not tight, and the tugs should lie in the middle of the pad. Only when you are going downhill with the weight of the vehicle resting on the breeching should the backband and tugs be pushed a little to the front of the pad and the traces allowed to hang loose.

## Problems with harnessing or vehicle balance

Most harnessing problems can be identified and put right before setting off but others, like vehicle balance, may not be apparent until the horse and vehicle are in motion. With the horse stood still, if the vehicle is drawn forward about 15 cm (6 in) the breeching should come into play. If the breeching is too loose, the weight of the vehicle will be taken on the backband when going downhill, and there may even be the danger of the vehicle touching the horse's hindquarters or, worse still, of the horse striking his hocks on the front of the vehicle when trotting. Shortening the breeching straps will maintain an adequate distance between the horse and the vehicle on the steepest of gradients. An over-tight breeching will prevent the horse moving properly, and it is important that the breeching is only operational on downhills or if the horse has to stop suddenly. If the tugs and backband do not lie perpendicular to the pad when travelling on level ground, the traces will need adjustment by lengthening them to prevent the tugs being pushed too far forward by the shafts, or shortening them to prevent the tugs being pulled back behind the pad. However, it should be remembered that shortening the traces tightens the breeching and vice versa so any adjustments to either the traces or breeching need to be done with due care for the other. The shaft height can be altered by raising or lowering the tugs on the backband and, if the bellyband is of the running type, a one hole adjustment on one side, which may be sufficient to achieve the desired effect, can be balanced by drawing the backband through its channel until the shafts lie at the same level. Balancing problems with two-wheeled vehicles can generally be sorted out by either altering the shaft height, moving the sliding seat in those vehicles like ralli cars, which have one, rearranging the seating position of the passengers with regard to their respective individual weights, or even carrying ballast in the form of a weight under the seat in the case of some gigs. Sometimes a combination of one or more of these methods will help achieve perfect balance with as little weight as possible pushing down on the horse's back or pressing up on the bellyband.

## Harnessing a Pair

The procedure for harnessing a pair is very similar to that for harnessing a single horse, and the harness for each horse of the pair will be nearly identical except for the collars, which may need to be a different size to ensure they fit the individual horses properly. Collars used in pair harness have a link, known as the kidney link on account of its shape, which connects the hames at the bottom, and on this link there is a floating ring to which the pole straps or chains are fastened. To make adjustments easier, the top hame straps have the buckles on the inside so that the points of the straps are drawn outwards and downwards to tighten or loosen them, which is easier than having to pull them upwards and inwards, especially if the horses are big. The hame tugs on a pair collar are longer than on a single harness collar so that the hame tug buckles lie in line with the pad when the horse is fully harnessed. After the collars have been put on, the false martingales, if used, are buckled around both the collar and the upper part of the kidney link, which helps to hold the hames in the groove of the collar.

As pair pads only have the weight of the traces to carry, they are much narrower and lighter than single harness pads and instead of a backband there is a metal dee below the terret on each side of each pad to which are sewn short leather straps. These straps are fastened to the buckles on the end of short leather straps sewn onto a dee ring on the top of the hame tug buckle. A strap sewn to the dee ring on the bottom of the hame tug buckle takes the bellyband, which has a buckle at either end. On some pair harness, the bellyband comprises a long strap, which is sewn to the bottom dee on the inside hame buckle, and there is a short strap terminating in a buckle on the outside hame tug buckle to which it fastens. With this method the hames are not interchangeable. The hame tugs are buckled to the straps on the pad and the bellyband is passed through the false martingale and fastened, but looser than would be the case with single harness. The traces are buckled on and laid across each horse's back in readiness for putting to with the outer trace of each horse on top. The trace ends, which attach to the vehicle, can be of several designs, the most common having a metal dee at the end through which the point of the trace is passed to form a running loop. Alternatively, the trace end may just be stitched back onto itself to form a simple loop, and there are several patterns of quick release trace end.

The bridles are put on next, and pair bridles are no different from single harness bridles except that if the noseband buckles are to one side they should be on the outside so that they can be easily reached for adjustment once the horses are put to. If Liverpool driving bits are used, they should have a bar across the bottom of the cheeks to prevent the horses getting the bit cheeks caught on the coupling rein or hooked up in the other horse's bridle.

The reins comprise draught reins which go from the nearside bit ring of the nearside horse and the offside bit ring of the offside horse direct to the driver, and coupling reins which are buckled to them. A series of holes in each draught rein enables the coupling rein to be adjusted. The nearside coupling rein passes through the inside hame terret of the nearside horse and across to the inside bit ring of the offside horse, and vice versa, so that when the right rein is pulled pressure is exerted on the right side of both mouths and the horses turn to the right. The reins are put on by passing them through the pad and hame terrets and tucking the loose end beyond the coupling buckles under the backstrap or through the pad terret. The draught rein can be buckled direct to the outside bit ring but the coupling rein cannot be fastened until both horses are in the vehicle, and should be passed around the back of the noseband or inside hame terret and pushed into the keeper but not buckled. It is usual to have the buckle on the end of the offside rein as, once the horses are put to, it will be necessary to throw the nearside rein over the horses' backs to the offside before mounting and if the buckle were on the nearside rein it could injure someone if it struck them in the face. Also, if the buckle rein is always on the offside, there is less danger of getting the reins on the wrong horse as coupling reins need careful adjustment and, once correctly adjusted, it is frustrating and time-wasting to have to keep altering them again every time the horses are put to.

## Putting to a Pair

Some pair harness has trace bearers, which are long adjustable straps that pass through a slot in each horse's backstrap and have a loop at either end through which the traces pass to give a tidier appearance. Breechings can also be used with pair harness and are especially useful in hilly country or if the vehicle does not have a brake. If breast collars are used, breechings are essential. Pair breechings are similar to full breeching on single harness except that the breeching straps are much longer and buckle into the hame tug buckles.

Before putting a pair to, the vehicle should be wheeled out into a suitable position on level ground and made ready by bolting the splinter bar into place, if not already done, and inserting the base of the pole through the bracket below the splinter bar and into the pole socket on the forecarriage. A bolt behind the splinter bar passes through the pole and prevents it moving. On those vehicles which can be used with shafts for a single horse too, the splinter bar is usually designed to bolt into the same brackets that held the shafts. The four roller bolts to which the traces are fastened are positioned on top of the splinter bar. The polestraps or chains should be fastened to the polehead on the end of the pole, then the horses can be led up from behind the vehicle to stand alongside the pole. If necessary, the horses can be quietly pushed sideways into position but they should never be backed into place as the horses cannot see where they are going and may hit the splinter bar. The polestraps or chains should be slipped through the kidney link rings on the collars and buckled loosely. Some people like to pass the polestrap through the kidney link and around the collar as well as a precaution against the hames being pulled off the collar in the event of an accident. The outside trace of each horse is fastened next, which prevents the horse swinging his quarters out from the vehicle, followed by the inside traces, which will necessitate learning over behind the horse. If there is any risk of one of the horses kicking, he should be put to first and his inside trace fastened from the pole side before the other is brought out.

Some vehicles have a pivotting swingle-

**26** Ms Christine Heaps driving her pair of part-bred greys to a phaeton. The wind-on brake mechanism is typical of vehicles built on the continent

tree for each horse's traces rather than a splinter bar and this arrangement allows the traces to give and take with each stride which keeps the collars lying flat on the shoulders and is more comfortable for the horses. Swingletrees are essential if breast collars are used. Some swingletrees have trace hooks on each end but others have triangular lugs over which the traces pass and a leather lace called a rat tail, which is attached to the swingletree, goes over the trace and through the hole in the lug to hold the trace in place. For both methods, single harness type traces with crew or dart holes in the end are used. The horses are 'poled up' next by shortening the polestraps or chains so that they keep the vehicle well clear of the horses' hocks but are not so tight that they pull continually on the horses' necks causing discomfort. There should always be a little 'play' so that if chains are used they jingle when the horses are in motion. As a safety precaution if chains are used, the spring hooks should be fastened downwards so that there is less risk of the crossbar of the bit getting caught in the hook. Lastly, the coupling reins are fastened, the horse with the highest head carriage having his on top. It may be necessary to buckle the reins onto plain cheek for one horse and middle bar for the other or to use a leather curb strap for one and a metal curb chain for the other in order to achieve an equal 'feel' on the horses' mouths. If rough cheek position is used for either horse, the coupling rein should be buckled around the cheekpiece only rather than around the bit ring as well which would cause the side of the bit to press in on the side of the horse's mouth. Occasionally, a brass or ivory coupling ring is used, and both coupling reins passed through it so that the ring lies where they cross and helps hold them together. If breeching is used, the breeching straps would have been buckled into the hame tug buckles under the traces before the horses were brought out to the vehicle.

## Driving a Single or Pair

Whether driving a single or a pair, before mounting the vehicle a final check should be made to ensure that everything is in order. Look to see if the traces are the correct length and properly secured to the vehicle, that the tugs are in front of the stops on the shafts, and the collar hames firmly in place and the hame straps tight. Check that the breeching is correctly adjusted, the bellyband at the right length and passed through the false martingale, the kicking strap if one is used not too tight, and the bridle properly fitted, paying particular attention to the bit and curb chain. With a pair, the pole straps and coupling reins will need checking too. Every buckle should be firmly secured, and every strap in its keeper.

Passengers should not mount the vehicle until the driver is seated and in full control, and the groom or assistant should remain standing at the horse's head until asked by the driver to step aside immediately prior to moving off. The whip should either be placed in the whip socket or, if this is likely to impede access as is often the case with whipholders attached to the right-hand side of the dashboard, laid up against the middle of the seat with the butt end resting against the base of the dashboard. Gloves should always be worn when driving as they give a better grip on the reins, and should be laid ready on the seat together with the driving apron. 'Dogskin' gloves are generally considered the best although any good quality leather gloves will be suitable if the leather is not too thick and they are unlined. For wet weather driving, wool or string gloves are preferable, as leather can become slippery when wet.

## Mounting the vehicle

To mount the vehicle **(Fig. 28)**, the driver should stand on the offside of the vehicle and with the right hand take the reins from the pad terret or from under the backstrap and buckle the ends together. Holding the reins still in the right hand with the nearside rein under the index finger and the offside rein under the middle finger with the buckled end looped over the little finger, the handle or rail on the dashboard should be firmly gripped between the thumb and index finger of the right hand while the left hand holds onto the handle on the vehicle body or the mudguard. A wise precaution is to have the offside rein a few inches longer than the nearside rein so that if the horse(s) moves suddenly before the driver is seated, both reins will be the same length and an even contact on the reins will help to keep

*Fig. 28* Mounting the vehicle – the driver stands on the offside, taking the reins in the right hand, with the nearside rein under the index finger and the offside rein under the middle finger. The handle on the dashboard is gripped between thumb and index finger of the right hand and the left hand holds the vehicle body or mudguard

the horse(s) straight. The right foot is placed on the step and the driver mounts quickly and quietly and sits down immediately, tucking the driving apron in around himself as he does so. The driver always sits on the offside of the vehicle as, if he sat on the nearside, every time he used his right hand on the reins or used the whip the passenger would get nudged with his elbow.

Some two-wheeled vehicles, especially high dogcarts, have two steps up but the procedure is the same, with the right foot placed on the lower step and the left foot on the higher step. When getting out of such a vehicle, it is important to remember to follow an exact reversal of the procedure for getting in by coming out backwards beginning with the left foot. Four-wheeled vehicles often have a step attached to the hub of the offside front wheel, and very high four-wheelers like brakes may have an additional step in the form of a small foot-plate on top of the offside outside roller bolt in which case the left foot is placed on the step and the right foot on the foot plate. Once again, the procedure is reversed to get out of the vehicle.

## Holding the reins and whip

As soon as the driver is seated, the reins should be transferred to the left hand with the nearside rein over the index finger and the offside rein under the middle finger with the free ends of the reins hanging down against the palm where they are held by the other fingers. The thumb should be kept level and pointing to the right. The right hand is then free to hold the whip at an angle of 45 degrees against the body and pointing slightly forward, to make hand signals, and to assist the left hand as and when required **(Fig. 29)**. At all times the reins should be kept together in the left hand but not gripped tightly, which would make the whole forearm rigid and unyielding. A light firm grip is required, and the hands should be held about 8 cm (3 in) in front of the body with the forearms roughly horizontal. The elbows should be kept close to the sides of the body with the back straight and the head up. The knees and feet should be close together and there must be sufficient legroom for the driver to be able to stretch his legs out so that the knees are just slightly bent when the feet are firmly up against the footboard. As adequate purchase for the feet is essential to give the driver security and to increase the potential leverage he is able to exert on the reins, a sloping footboard is preferable to a flat floor. Some vehicles are fitted with an adjustable footrest, which can be especially useful if people of differing height and length of leg drive the same vehicle.

A low driving seat restricts visibility, limits the effectiveness of the driver, and looks unworkmanlike, apart from being uncomfortable although additional cushions or a 'wedge' seat can make a great improvement. Too high a seat with inadequate purchase for the feet can be equally dangerous as if the horse shies or moves suddenly or the vehicle hits a pothole in the road the driver can be rocked from this precarious position.

## The aids and how to give them

After the driver is seated and in control and the passengers have climbed into the vehicle and are safely seated, the driver can signal by way of a nod that he is ready and the assistant holding the horse can step out of the way. The office to move off can be given by feeling gently on the horse's mouth before asking him to 'walk on.' A light, even contact with the horse's mouth is essential and by giving a little with the hand when the horse steps forward from a halt the even feel will be maintained. Rigid hands, which jab a sensitive horse in the mouth when moving off, will soon make the horse cautious and liable to either jib or hesitate then leap forward into his collar in a bold attempt to avoid having his mouth hurt.

For the first kilometre (half mile) or so the horse should just be walked, which teaches him to set off quietly and gives the driver an opportunity to check that the vehicle is properly balanced if it is a two-wheeler and that the harness is correctly adjusted. If everything is satisfactory then

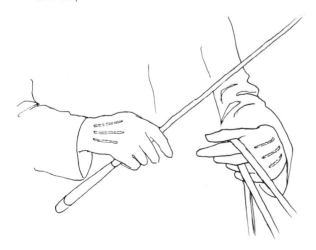

Fig. 29 Correct method of holding single or pair reins and whip

**27** Mrs E. Newboult-Young driving her Dartmoor pony stallion, Brandsby Cyclone, in the dressage phase of a combined driving event in Cherbourg, France. The movement is a 20 m circle with the reins held in the left hand only

a light feel on the reins followed by the command 'trot on' can be given. Verbal commands must be clear and decisive and backed up by the whip drawn lightly across his shoulder in front of the pad if he fails to respond. Increasing the pace can be achieved by repeating the verbal command, using a different tone of voice if required.

The principles of driving are the same for both a single horse or a pair except that with the latter both animals must be made to do their share of the work. Very often, one horse will do the bulk of the work while the other hangs back in his traces and the driver must send the lazy horse on into his collar. Pair reins also spread more from the hand and are heavier especially if the horses are inclined to pull.

By keeping the left hand and wrist supple, sufficient pressure should be able to be exerted on each rein individually by flexing the wrist to turn a well-trained and responsive horse (27). If the hand is turned so that the back of the hand is uppermost, the nearside rein will be pulled sufficiently to turn the horse to the left and, likewise, if the palm is turned uppermost the offside rein will be pulled to turn the horse to the right. Unless specifically making turns with one hand only, such as turning at a road junction when the right hand is signalling with the whip, the left hand should neither move to left nor right to increase the pressure on the rein. Normally, the right hand is used to assist the left in making a turn by being placed a little in front of the left hand and over the appropriate rein upon which pressure is put. By placing the right hand over both the reins with the nearside rein between the middle and third fingers and the offside rein under the little finger, assistance can be given to the left hand in holding a horse which pulls or, if the right hand takes the contact with the horse's mouth, to shorten or lengthen the reins by sliding the left hand up or down the slack rein behind the right hand. The position of the whip in the right hand must never change, and the whip should never be used while the right hand is on the reins. To decrease pace or stop, even and gradual pressure should be applied to the reins and the appropriate verbal command given. As soon as the horse has obeyed, the pressure on the reins must be relaxed and a light contact with the mouth resumed.

When trotting, a steady rhythmic pace should be the aim, with the horse relaxed and settled. Constant changes of pace are unnecessarily tiring for the horse. Depending on his size and natural length of stride, a trotting speed of 9–13 kph (6–8 mph) is a reasonable road pace. On slippery road surfaces, uneven ground or when negotiating corners, the pace should be decreased, and when approaching junctions or traffic lights the horse should be asked to walk and, if necessary, 'whoa' and 'stand.' Constant use of the same commands is essential if the horse is expected to learn and respond to them. If driving on public roads, the hand signals used and understood by motorists should be used but remembering that, as a horse-drawn vehicle moves considerably slower than a car, motorists have less time to see and comprehend the hand signals given from a carriage before they are upon it. In

**28** Mrs Heather Gow driving her Highland pony mare, Skye of Alltnacailleach, to a modern competition vehicle during the marathon phase of a combined driving event in Scotland

view of the traffic on modern roads, extra care must be taken by anyone driving a horse on a public road, bearing in mind that narrow country lanes with blind corners are often more dangerous than busy but open main roads.

## Driving up and down hills

It is safest always to descend hills at a walk so that there is less risk of the weight of the vehicle on the breeching causing the horse to slip. If the vehicle has a brake, this should be used with discretion by transferring the whip to the left hand so that the right hand is free to operate the brake lever to ease the weight on the horse. With a pair, the brake should be applied gently as soon as the pole has run forward sufficiently to tighten the pole straps or chains. Uphill gradients should be tackled at a trot and it is wise to increase the pace slightly when approaching a hill to produce a little more impetus. Only on very steep hills with a heavy vehicle should the horses be allowed to put in a few strides of canter or 'spring the hill' and even this is really undesirable with a horse in single harness. It is preferable to ask the passengers to get out and walk to the top of the hill, or to stop and rest the horse for a few minutes if the hill is long. Backing one wheel into the curbstone or placing a 'chock' behind the wheel will take the weight off his shoulders.

## The importance of good 'hands'

In driving, good hands are as important as in riding but, in maintaining an even contact with the horse's mouth, it should be remembered that the length of driving reins increases their weight and therefore sympathetic hands are very important. A light feel on the reins before turning, as with moving off, will alert the horse to a forthcoming command and concentrate his attention. The reins should be used in such a way that the contact is never lost, and pressure on one or both reins is exerted in a smooth, continuous action and relaxed as soon as the change of pace or direction is successfully achieved. Inconsistent contact or jerking the reins is bad practice as proper control cannot be maintained, and a young horse or one with a sensitive mouth can soon be ruined. It is important that if the driving whip is used, it is correctly applied between the pad and the collar. It is quite wrong and potentially dangerous to strike a horse on the hindquarters with the stock of the whip as, apart from encouraging the horse to kick, the whip can be damaged or broken. The skill required to 'place' a driving whip accurately is what gave rise to the term 'whip' for someone who drives horses. A driving whip should never be cracked like a hunting whip as this would probably snap or bend the goosequill in the end, and it is slovenly and ineffective to drive with the whip stuck in the whip socket on the vehicle. With regular practice, the necessary skills needed to handle driving reins and whip competently will be learnt and, once acquired, will never be forgotten.

## Unharnessing

To take a horse out of a vehicle, the procedure for putting to is exactly reversed. The passengers dismount first, followed by the driver who tucks the ends of the reins through the offside pad terret or, with a pair, unbuckles the ends and throws the nearside rein over the horse's backs to be bucked through the nearside pad terret. The bellyband is undone, then the breeching straps unbuckled and, lastly, the traces are unhooked before the vehicle is pushed back from the horse, making sure the shafts come clear of the tugs and the reins are not caught on the tug stop. The horse should not be led out of

29  Mr Les McCall driving his Dales pony, Barmston
Lad, to a spindle-back gig. The raised 'wedge' seat
used to raise the position of the driver can be seen
through the spindles of the seat back

the shafts, as an impatient horse can be
tempted to step forward too soon, causing
the shafts to fall from the tugs and possibly
break. With a pair, the coupling reins
should be unfastened first, then the traces
and, finally, the pole straps before the
horses are led forwards and outwards
away from the pole. With pairs, always
unfasten the inside traces before the outside traces. Unharnessing is again a
straight reversal of the procedure for
harnessing up, not forgetting to slip the
bellyband and girth out of the false martingale loop before lifting the pad from the
horse's back, and unfastening the curb
chain before sliding off the bridle.

## SUMMARY

**When driving:**
- Always hold the reins in the left hand
- Always carry a whip
- Never drive without an assistant
- Never allow your attention to be distracted
- Always have an assistant hold the horse until the driver is in the vehicle, seated and in control of the horse
- Passengers should not be allowed in the vehicle until the driver is seated and ready

**When harnessing and unharnessing:**
- Never attempt to back the horse between the shafts that are lying on the ground
- Never harness or unharness a horse without a capable assistant at his head
- Never take the bridle off while the horse is still harnessed to the vehicle
- Never leave a horse unattended, even for a moment, while it is harnessed to the vehicle
- Never begin to harness or unharness a horse without the reins attached to the bridle

# 6

# PROBLEMS AND HOW TO DEAL WITH THEM

## *Dealing with Problems in the Horse*

It is inevitable that every newcomer to driving will encounter some problems sooner or later. In many cases, the problem will be minor and the result of inexperience, such as having difficulty holding the reins correctly in the left hand. However, perseverance and practice will eventually make it second nature and the driver will be more effective and competent as a result. It is a mistake to set off driving with a rein in each hand thinking the correct method of holding the reins can be adopted later as bad habits are as difficult to cure with humans as with horses and, if the correct method is rigidly adhered to from the very start and a driving whip always carried in the right hand, any initial difficulties will soon be overcome.

Other problems, like incorrect harnessing, need to be worked at, checking the adjustment of each strap and buckle until experience enables the driver to see at a glance if the tugs are too low or the traces too long or the breeching too slack. Often by thinking the problem out logically the solution will be obvious, and it is useful to have in the mind's eye a picture of a correctly 'put to' turnout to use as a rough guide.

## Pulling

It is probably true to say that more problems are linked directly to the horse's mouth and bitting than anything else. A horse that pulls constantly is unpleasant and tiring to drive, and the problem is not always solved by using a more severe bit or buckling the reins lower on the cheeks of a curb bit to increase the leverage and severity.

Sometimes a severe bit can be the cause of a horse pulling, and he will be happier and more responsive in a milder bit. Finding the most suitable bit for a horse can be something of a trial and error process until one is found in which he will go kindly. Always begin the process with the mildest bit, or what he has been driven in previously, and use that as a base line from which to progress until the most suitable bitting arrangement has been found. The height of the bit in the horse's mouth, the position of the reins, the type of curb chain and its adjustment, and the 'hands' of the driver all have an important bearing on how the horse will react. Some bits have the mouthpiece roughened on one side and smooth on the other so that it can be used either way to vary the action; slightly curved or 'mullen' mouthpieces or those with tongue grooves or 'cherry rollers' along the mouthpiece are other variations **(Fig. 30)**. Bits with high ports

*Fig. 30* Bit with cherry rollers

are best left to more experienced horse-men as should horses that are confirmed and hardened pullers.

Some horses pull because they evade the bit by opening their mouths, and tighten-ing the noseband will often cure the fault. An independent noseband with its own supporting strap is often more effective than the usual type of driving noseband, which pulls the upper cheeks of the bit in when tightened and cannot be altered in height because it is fastened to the cheek-pieces on the bridle. Inadequate breaking and initial training can also be the cause of a horse pulling out of ignorance or lack of understanding, and a series of re-mou-thing lessons can help to re-educate a spoilt mouth, especially if supported by sympathetic 'hands' and good driving practice. Some horses always set off on a drive by taking hold but settle after a short distance, if the driver gives and takes with his hands and avoids the dead pull on the reins that is the cause of many difficult pullers.

## Head throwing

Regular checks of the horse's teeth should be made by slipping two fingers along the inside of the cheeks to see if there are any sharp edges as the discomfort caused by teeth in need of filing can cause horses to

pull, carry their heads to one side, or fuss constantly, and the problem is easily solved by a horse dentist or a veterinary surgeon with a tooth rasp. A badly-fitting bridle can also result in a horse throwing his head about, or it could be that the horse has a sensitive tooth irritated by the metal bit and by using a bit with a rubber or vulcanite mouthpiece or covering the mouthpiece in chamois leather the horse is no longer troubled.

## Tongue over the bit

Some horses develop the habit of evading the bit by getting the tongue over the mouthpiece, a habit which can emanate from having the bit too low in the mouth during training. Once the tongue is over the bit, the mouthpiece is forced down onto the bars of the mouth, which are sensitive, and the horse often reacts by jibbing, running backwards or, at the very least, not going forward into his bridle. There are various bits with devices attached to the mouthpiece to prevent the horse getting his tongue over, or a har-dened rubber tongue plate can be fastened to the mouthpiece so that it lies flat on the tongue at the back of the mouth and keeps the tongue in place **(Fig. 31)**. The great

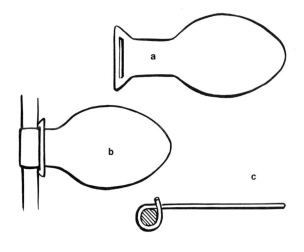

*Fig. 31* **a** Rubber tongue plate **b** on bit **c** side view

advantage of a tongue plate is that it can be removed and used on most bits with a straight mouthpiece, and it cannot be seen, which could be a consideration with a show horse. The old-fashioned method of tying the tongue down with a thin leather strap buckled around the lower jaw is less effective and can encourage the horse to fuss even more with its head, apart from being unsightly and advertising the horse's problem for all to see.

## Carrying the head to one side

A horse that carries his head on one side may do so because of a sharp molar in need of rasping or it could be because the bars on one side of his mouth are sore in which case a rest from work will usually solve the problem. A piece of thick, soft chamois leather stitched around the mouthpiece should prevent sore bars occurring again. Driving with uneven reins will also make a horse carry his head to one side but if the driver makes sure that the stitching where the two strips of leather making up each rein are spliced are level when driving, the problem should not arise. Inconsistent or jerking contact on the reins can make a horse throw his head up or carry it high with the nose thrust forward to avoid the jabbing in his mouth.

## Going heavy on the forehand

It is a misconception, especially among the riding fraternity, that driving makes a horse heavy on the forehand when ridden. There is no truth in this at all as if a horse is properly driven with his hocks well under him his head will, as a consequence, be carried in the right place and he will be balanced and light in hand to drive. A horse that has any tendency to go on the

**30** Work on the lunge, in long reins and under saddle, can help to balance the horse

forehand can be improved by balancing exercises, including working him on the lunge, in long-reins and under saddle to encourage him to use his hindquarters and lift his head as a result **(25)**. Balancing exercises can sometimes be more effectively achieved under saddle as the rider's legs provide a more direct aid than the driver's voice and whip in mustering the necessary impulsion. The hands should provide a light but consistent contact, and once the horse is 'between hand and leg' under saddle the work can be progressed and practised in harness.

## Skipping and breaking pace

Some riding horses when driven are inclined to skip when 'sent on' at a trot but constant correction will usually help the horse to differentiate between work under saddle when he may be required to canter, gallop and jump, and work between shafts when he is only required to walk or trot. If the problem continues, the vehicle may be too heavy and the horse could be skipping to increase momentum in which case a lighter vehicle should be the answer. Alternatively, the horse may be too immature or insufficiently fit for the work required of him, or he may simply be tired and skipping is the symptom of it.

## Cold-shouldered

A cold-shouldered horse is one that is reluctant to set off and may play up or even run backwards rather than take the weight in his collar and move forward. A badly-fitting collar, which has caused sore shoulders, could be the culprit, and a rest followed by a change to a properly fitting collar should help. A breast collar is a useful standby for such occasions. Other possible causes of sore shoulders could be using a breast collar without a swingletree, a jolt to the shoulders caused by the

vehicle striking a solid object like a rock during a cross-country marathon, or dirt and sweat left on the collar rubbing and causing a gall. Serge or wool-lined collars need to be thoroughly dried and brushed after each time they are used. Thin-skinned horses are more prone to sore shoulders but a little surgical spirit rubbed over the shoulders can help to harden the skin. Using a vehicle that is too heavy can also cause a horse to jib, as can failing to give with the hand to allow the horse to lower his head when moving off, which soon results in a horse hesitant to move for fear of a jab in the mouth. Turning the horse to one side to set off will often get around the problem, or the horse can even be led to get it moving, which will encourage a quiet and calm start. Under no circumstances should the problem be tackled with force by shouting or using the whip as this is only likely to compound the situation and upset the horse even more. Avoid halting and moving off on hills where the weight of the vehicle will be increased by the gradient, and if possible wait until the horse is walking on before the groom or assistant mounts so that the starting weight of the vehicle is kept to a minimum. Regular checks of the shoulders should be made to ensure there are no areas of soreness developing before they become a problem, and for the same reason periodic examinations of the mouth, especially the bars, are advisable.

## Kicking

Horses with a tendency to kick or rear are unsuitable for a novice driver. However, a horse which kicks unexpectedly and out of character could be doing so for a particular reason, which may be easily dealt with before the occurrence has become a habit

31  Mrs Georgina Turner driving Mr Roger Bass's Hackney stallion, Theydon Saffron, to a spindle-back gig

116

and the horse branded a confirmed kicker. Incorrect harnessing, which permits the breeching to ride up under the tail or the vehicle to touch the horse, is the most usual cause of kicking, but bad driving practice in the form of slapping the reins on the horse's hindquarters or using the stock of the whip to strike the horse behind the pad are other possible inducements to kick. Conversely, a horse may kick because the crupper is too tight or has rubbed his dock, which is why regular examination of the horse while grooming is as important as making sure the harness fits properly. Using a kicking strap will not prevent a horse kicking completely but will limit the movement of his hind legs and consequently the damage to the vehicle and harness. If a horse in pair harness kicks and gets a leg over the pole, it is safer to unharness both horses and lead the offender down the pole than to try and lift the leg over which could upset the horse even more. With a leg over a trace, the trace should be unfastened, taking care the horse does not kick out again, and refastened correctly.

## Rearing

Rearing is a dangerous vice and no horse so disposed is safe to be put between shafts. Occasionally, keen and corned-up driving horses will tend to get impatient and lift their forefeet slightly off the ground in their eagerness to move off when halted at road junctions, and care must be taken to prevent enthusiasm getting out of hand and becoming a habit then a vice. During all stages of training, the horse must be taught to stand still when required. Time and patience instilling and practising this lesson will pay dividends in the long run as a horse that will stand to be harnessed, put to, in the line-up at a show, at road junctions and so forth will be considerably more pleasant

to handle than one that requires two people to hold it still when halted. If the practice of always walking the first and last kilometre (half mile) of a drive is rigidly adhered to, horses will be encouraged to set off and return home calmly and without rushing.

Insufficient work and too much hard feed cause many problems and the old saying that a horse should only be fed what he earns is very true. If for any reason the horse is not being worked one day, his feed should be proportionately reduced and, in the case of stabled animals, he should be turned out for a couple of hours in a field to get some exercise and to prevent him becoming bored.

## Shying

Shying at objects, imagined or real, in the side of the road is an irritating habit, which can also be dangerous if driving in busy traffic on public roads. Young horses that shy from inexperience and over-cautiousness generally grow out of the habit as they get older, and horses that shy from sheer exuberance when first taken out for exercise usually settle after a while and get on with their job. Persistent shying, however, may be attributable to a badly fitting bridle that allows the horse to see out of the back of the blinkers, or it could even be defective vision, which makes it difficult for the horse to discern objects clearly and therefore raises his natural suspiciousness. Occasionally, a horse that shies badly in a blinkered bridle will be perfectly well mannered if re-trained to go in an open bridle, although it is imperative to accustom him to the open bridle in gradual stages or he may be frightened of the moving wheels behind him.

32   Mrs Mary Dutton driving her Welsh Cob mare, Heathey Morena, through a watersplash hazard

## Leaning in pair harness

Horses in pair harness sometimes pick up the habit of leaning away from the pole, which looks unsightly and can be dangerous on slippery roads as the horses are more likely to lose their footing. One cause is having the pole straps too tight so that the horses are encouraged to go that way by pressure from the collars, or incorrect adjustment of the coupling rein could be to blame. Occasionally, the problem is reversed and the horses turn their heads outwards and lean against the pole. If the harness is properly fitted and has not rubbed the horses or caused soreness, in which case they may not be going straight to avoid the pressure of the harness, periodically altering the side of the pole the individual horses work on may solve the problem. In extreme cases, a small oblong pad with short bristles attached to the pole or trace will often discourage the horse from leaning that way. Using a pair vehicle without a brake or breeching can cause soreness on the top of the necks where the collars are pulled down with great pressure by the action of the pole against the pole straps, and the horses may go unevenly or with reluctance as a result. A horse that will not go straight in single harness usually does so because of inexperience, bad harnessing or ineffective driving.

## Jibbing in pair harness

Sometimes a horse will jib in pair harness because of being a keener and more responsive animal than his co-worker. When the office to 'walk on' is given, the keener horse steps forward and is thwarted by the other horse, which is slower to move forward and holds him back. The result is a shambling, uneven start, which can soon lead to the keener horse being hesitant to set off as he expects to be immediately held back then hauled forward when the lazier horse moves. The solution is to make sure both horses move off at the same time by drawing the whip across the lazy horse's shoulders as the command to 'walk on' is given. The same procedure should also be used when making the transition from walk to trot, and at all times the lazier horse must be made to do his fair share of the work.

## Slipping on the road

Some road surfaces, especially lime-stone chips, which become polished with wear, can be very slippery and if a horse has to be driven regularly on such roads it may be necessary to use some form of non-slip shoeing as a precaution against him losing his footing and coming down on the road. At one time, it was common practice to have calkins on the outer or both heels of the hind shoes and, by turning the tips of the shoe down to form the calkins, a better foothold was given (**Fig. 32**). If the calkins were only on the outer heels of the hind shoes, the inside heels were brought to a similar level by thickening them to form wedges. Calkins wear down very quickly, and it is possible for a horse to injure himself on them when lying down in the stable or field, and large calkins that raise the heel and set the hoof at an unnatural angle put a strain on the tendons if the horse is worked on the hard road. A safer

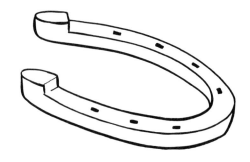

*Fig. 32* Horse shoe with calkins

*Fig. 33* Horse show with studs

and more effective system is to use studs, small, hardened metal plugs, sometimes with a centre core of exceptionally hard metal, which are screwed or tapped into holes specially drilled or punched into the corners of each shoe **(Fig. 33)**. Often a stud in the outer heel of each hind shoe, with the inner heel 'wedged' to maintain the same level, will be sufficient to give the horse extra grip on slippery roads. The great advantage of studs is that they are easy to fit, hard wearing, and can be left in the shoes until the horse needs reshoeing and, being small, they also put no strain on the tendons by substantially altering the angle of the foot.

## Driving in snow

In winter, snow can become packed in the hoofs, making it difficult for the horse to keep his feet; but thickly smearing the soles of the hoofs with grease will prevent snow balling. On icy roads, studs will again help to maintain a grip on the most slippery surface, and they are preferable to frost nails or 'sharps', which are hard, chisel-headed nails fitted in place of ordinary nails in the shoes but which wear quickly. When driving on slippery road surfaces, reduce the pace, especially on corners, and on bad hills if passengers get out and walk, there is less risk of the

weight of the vehicle causing the horse's legs to slip from beneath him.

As driving horses do far more of their work on the roads than most riding horses, their shoes wear out more quickly and for this reason a heavier road shoe is often favoured. Excessively heavy shoes are unnecessary, however, as they tend to encourage the horse to shorten his length of stride and use more knee and hock action because of the extra weight he has to lift with each step. Regular visits from the farrier are very important. He will fit new shoes or remove the old shoes to pare the hoof down before replacing the same set if not unduly worn, and will prevent many potential problems caused by neglect of the feet actually occurring. Very often poor action in horses is as a direct result of sore feet or bad shoeing, and a good remedial farrier will probably be able to put the problem right in a few visits. Stumbling may be due to bad shoeing, tiredness or lazy action, or it may be due to a weak heart and veterinary advice should be sought. Poor, shuffling action can be improved by working the horse over poles on the ground either on the lunge or under saddle to encourage him to lengthen his stride, and by sending him forward into his bridle when he is driven so that he really uses his hind legs and his head is raised and flexed at the poll in response to the light contact on the reins. A horse that lopes along with his head held low is unable to stride out with his back legs.

Specialist show horse trainers use a variety of methods to improve action including 'rattlers' or small hardwood balls threaded onto a thin leather strap which is loosely buckled around the fetlocks to encourge a rhythmic and more animated action. Weighted shoes and elasticated 'action developers' are similarly used to produce a flashier way of going for the showring, while various forms of 'dumb jockeys', draw-reins and devices using pulleys are intended to improve the head carriage. Attaching small, running, lead weights on hooks to the bit rings when the horse is standing in the stable encourage him to flex at the poll so that the weights are bearing down on the poll through the cheekpieces of the bridle and not on the bars of the mouth as they would be if the head were in the normal position. All these methods produce an artificial effect, which is unnecessary outside the professional showring.

## Problems with Vehicles

### Balancing a two-wheeled vehicle

Of the problems associated with vehicles, incorrect balance with a two-wheeler is probably the most common but it can usually be easily rectified by redistributing the weight over the axle by moving the seat forwards or backwards, re-arranging the seating position of the passengers, or altering the shaft height in the tugs. Sometimes a vehicle that appears perfectly balanced at a standstill vibrates violently when the horse is trotting on. This is generally caused by incorrect balance, and a slight adjustment of the tug height up or down should prevent the action of the horse being transmitted through the shafts to the passengers. While the bellyband should be slack enough to allow the shafts some movement through the tugs, it should not be so loose that when going uphill the shafts are so 'light on' that they point skyward and the whole vehicle is tilted backwards.

**33** Mr J. Sharpe driving Navarre, a Friesian stallion, to a meadowbrook. By having the axle actually inside the vehicle, it is possible to have the seats at shaft height and maintain a low centre of gravity

## Adjusting the height of a vehicle

If the vehicle is too small for the horse, the addition of a wooden block between the spring and axle on either side will raise the height by up to about 10 cm (4 in) or, alternatively, if the wheels are removed and a larger pair substituted, but with the same type and size of box fitting, a similar result may be achieved. However, by changing the size of the wheels, the overall symmetry of the vehicle could be spoilt, and it may be necessary to alter the position of the steps, mudguards and lamp brackets to accommodate the larger wheels. Reducing the size of the wheels to lower the height of the vehicle can make the body look out of proportion and over-large, while the 'drag' factor is increased by the smaller wheels in relation to the same body weight as when the larger wheels were used.

34 A Welsh Mountain pony driven to a Morgan-Davies exercise cart. Indispension units fitted between the stub axles and the body provide the suspension for these vehicles

## Problems with shafts

Shafts that are too short can easily be replaced with longer ones although altering the front of the vehicle to widen the shafts can be a more complicated job. By removing a pair of straight shafts and replacing them with curved shafts, the vehicle will accommodate a larger horse without raising the height of the body. Shaft furnishings, like tug stops and breeching dees, that are not in the right place can easily be unscrewed and moved as necessary.

**35** A Shetland pony driven to a cab-fronted gig in a novelty obstacle driving class. Cab shafts allow the vehicle to be built low to the ground, facilitating easy access, without altering the shaft height for the pony

36 Miss S. Dixon driving her crossbred mare, Donna, to a ralli car. Some ralli cars were built with the shafts inside the body which permitted the vehicle to be built wider but generally gave a less comfortable ride

## Carrying spares

In the event of any part of the harness breaking, it is wise to carry 'spares' so that running repairs can be made and the turnout is not incapacitated if out on a drive. Standard spares should include a trace, a rein, a hame strap, and a quantity of strong cord and a sharp knife. A spare pole strap should be carried on pair turnouts, and a hoof pick is a useful addition in case the horse picks up a stone in a shoe. The spares should be kept together in a box or waterproof bag under the seat to prevent them rolling forward and getting in the driver's feet or slipping out of the back if the vehicle has a let-down tailboard like a dogcart.

## Tipping over

Possibly the most dangerous thing that can happen when driving is to turn the vehicle over. The cause could be careless driving in allowing one wheel to get into a ditch or up the banking at the side of a road, or it could be as a result of a breaking shaft, a wheel coming off, or even just something startling the horse, which leaps sideways causing the vehicle to topple over. Obviously, the higher the vehicle and the narrower the track width, the greater the risk, but regular checks for loose bolts, slack wheels, cracked shafts, worn spring shackles and so forth could prevent an unnecessary accident.

In the event of a broken shaft, lost wheel or turn-over, the first priority must be to regain control of the horse as soon as possible by establishing contact with the reins until someone can get to his head. The horse should then be unharnessed from the vehicle, using the correct method, as quickly as possible. It is dangerous to try and right a vehicle when the horse is still attached to it. If the horse is brought down in an accident, it may be safer to keep him on the ground by sitting gently on his head, making sure his eye lying against the ground is protected from injury either by the blinker or by cupping one hand over it until the vehicle is removed. If the harness has to be cut to get the vehicle clear, it should be the stitching rather than the leather which is cut as the stitching will be easier, quicker and less expensive to sever using the knife out of the spares box on the vehicle.

If a horse has been involved in an accident, he will inevitably be frightened and, while it is important to get him back in harness as soon as possible, great care should be taken as if he is unsettled he will be more liable either to kick or try to take off. In accidents where the bridle has come off and the horse is therefore likely to bolt, control is best re-established by getting the bridle back on as quickly as possible. In emergencies, a coat placed over the horse's head as a blindfold can help to keep him under control until the bridle is replaced or the horse unharnessed from the vehicle. As a precaution, some people like to have a strong nylon headcollar under the bridle when driving at home or on rallies so that they have something to hold onto if such an occurrence happens, and a headcollar and lead-rope is always a useful addition to have in the spares box when out on drives. In dealing with any emergencies or accidents, remain calm and deal with the problem quickly and methodically.

## Safety precautions

Safety when driving is largely a matter of common sense, but it is worth bearing in mind the main causes of accidents with a driving turnout so that problems may be avoided. Failing to follow the rules for putting to and taking out, incorrect harnessing, and using defective harness or a vehicle that is not roadworthy can all lead to accidents, but other causes can be driving a horse that is insufficiently trained or unsuitable for harness work because of its temperament or a specific vice, like kicking.

However, the major cause is bad driving in the form of carelessness or irresponsibility, excessive speed, turning too sharply especially on slippery roads, tipping the vehicle at too sharp an angle, not concentrating and allowing the attention to be distracted, and failing to maintain control of the horse at all times. An alert driver is likely to be able to anticipate things that may frighten his horse and, by reducing speed and talking to him, avert possible problems. Always keep the reins in the left hand as it is impossible to shorten the reins quickly if they are held separately in each hand, and a momentary loss of control could permit the horse to shy into a ditch, turn around in the road or even take off. The whip must always be carried as it may be necessary to use it quickly to send a hesitant horse forward to avoid trouble. With a young or inexperienced horse, an agile assistant who can jump down and give assistance from the ground is very useful, and at no time should passengers get into a vehicle before the driver or should the driver dismount before the passengers.

On the roads, the horse should be kept in to the side and with a safe distance between it and other turnouts if driving in company. Hand signals should be clearly given to those behind when turning, slowing down or stopping, and overtaking should be done with great care and at a sensible speed and not too close, and if the horse being overtaken gets alarmed or excited draw back quietly until it has

settled down again. Never leave a horse unattended, never tie up a horse still harnessed to the vehicle, and never take the bridle off before the horse is out of the vehicle as this inevitably results in a frightened horse and a nasty accident. The damage a terrified horse can do dragging a vehicle on its side behind him, especially on a busy road or on a showfield, is horrendous and need never happen if correct procedures and accident prevention rules are followed.

## SUMMARY

***The most common causes of accidents are:***
- Lack of knowledge or experience on the part of the driver
- Inexperience or lack of training of the horse
- Defective harness or vehicle
- Incorrect harnessing
- Carelessness or distraction of the driver
- Lack of competent assistance

***On drives it is advisable to carry:***
- Spares (a rein, trace, hame strap, strong cord and a knife)
- A headcollar and lead rope
- A hoofpick

**37** Mr G.T. Heard's Welsh Cob, Crossroads Captain Courageous, driven to a side-bar runabout. These vehicles are only suitable for certain types of driving activity because of the restricted front-wheel lock due to the design of the body

# 7
# COMPETING WITH A DRIVING TURNOUT

## Competitive Driving

Most people who take up driving will at some stage try driving competitively, even if it is only to support the local show or a novice event organized by their local driving club. Apart from the opportunity to make comparative assessments of the quality of their turnout including the training and performance of the horse and their own skill as a *whip*, competing can give their involvement in the sport a focal point and clear objectives in terms of achievement levels and timescales. It will also provide opportunities to socialise with other driving enthusiasts, and many people compete as much for the fun of participating as for the chance of winning.

### Preparing the horse for competition

As competitive driving of any kind means driving in the company of other turnouts, from a safety point of view it is important to make sure the horse is properly trained and adequately experienced, especially if he is young or newly broken, before being taken to a show or event as most horses find their first outing in company an

38 Warming up. The vehicle in the foreground is an American road cart

exciting experience. A non-competitive and informal rally is the ideal place to take a young horse to gain experience in the company of other horses and, to get maximum benefit from the outing, it is best to arrive early so that the horse can be unboxed and led around to see the other turnouts and what is going on. This will also give him time to settle down before he is put to and quietly walked around prior to everyone setting off on the drive. It is a mistake to be the last turnout to leave the field or wherever the meet is held as the last horse in a line always has to work harder than the rest to keep up, and a young horse who thinks he is being left behind may be encouraged to pull, constantly break pace or even play up. If possible, position him between two quiet and sensible horses, keeping plenty of room in between, and concentrate on getting him to go in a relaxed and responsive manner. He will probably be inclined to try and get too close to the horse and vehicle in front but once he realizes he is not slipping behind, he should settle and maintain a steady pace. If the line of horses and vehicles slows down or has to stop for any reason, avoid getting him penned in between other turnouts by leaving enough room all round so that if he becomes uneasy and misbehaves there is no danger of him backing into the horse behind or jumping forward into the vehicle in front. It is better to ask the groom to get down and hold him than to try and control him from the vehicle if he is young and inexperienced and there is limited room.

After a few outings to rallies, if the horse is unperturbed by other turnouts, including being overtaken (which may upset him as he will be unable to see the other horse coming from behind), and is not frightened by traffic, spectators or everyday objects at the side of the road, then he should be ready for his first show or competitive event. The local driving club will probably produce a programme of activities for the year or there may be a driving class at one of the local agricultural or horse shows but, in choosing a suitable competitive debut for the horse, select a venue where there is plenty of room and where there will not be too many people or other horses. Agricultural shows and fairs, apart from being crowded and noisy, sometimes also host such attractions as hot air balloons, motorcycle display teams or steam engines, which could terrify a novice horse, and a specialist driving show is likely to be a more suitable environment. The venue chosen should be within reasonable travelling distance, and the date of the show should allow sufficient time to get the horse fit and ready, and to make other preparations as necessary.

Study the show schedule carefully and select those classes in which to compete, avoiding the temptation to enter every class for which the horse is eligible in preference to those for which the horse is most suited. If in doubt about any part of the show schedule, telephone the secretary for clarification. Before posting entries, remember to draw a circle around the class numbers on the schedule as this will avoid the embarrassment of forgetting which classes the horse has been

entered in. It can be a useful reference to note the date of posting in a corner of the schedule. Most importantly, put the schedule somewhere safe where it cannot be lost and, if the show passes and exhibitors' numbers are posted out to competitors by the secretary prior to the show, put them with the schedule as soon as they are received.

## Private Driving Classes

Show classes are generally referred to as 'private driving' classes (pleasure driving classes in the U.S.), the entries being limited to owner-driven private vehicles, such as gigs or dogcarts, as opposed to coachman-driven vehicles like broughams or trade vehicles like butchers' carts or milk floats. Some of the larger shows stage special trade turnout classes. The criteria by which private driving classes are judged are based on the fundamental rules handed down by previous generations who

**39** Mr C.R. Darley's Fell pony, Flimby Hall Grey Cloud, driven to a cee-spring gig during the judging of a private driving class

40 Mr and Mrs R. Stoddart's Welsh Cob stallion, Regency Teddy, driven to a dogcart by Barbara Stoddart. This famous driving horse has won 85 first prizes and 29 championships in private driving classes

drove horses for business and pleasure, and the judge will be looking for a turnout that is traditional in style, correctly assembled, immaculately clean, road-worthy, and a pleasure to drive. Each part of the turnout will be assessed individually then as a whole to ensure it gives a pleasing overall effect. An ideal private driving horse will be as near perfect in conformation as possible with substance and straight, ground-covering action, and bold but well mannered and responsive making him suitable for an amateur to drive in safety. As exaggerated action is not required, Hackneys are debarred from most private driving classes. A horse which will stand still when required without having to be held is a great asset in the showring.

41  A wheelchair-bound exhibitor competing in the disabled driver class, British Driving Society Show

## Harness and vehicle

The harness must fit properly and be clean and supple and of a suitable type to match the horse and vehicle. Trade harness would be incorrect in a private driving class, and very fine 'skeleton' harness or heavy vanner-type harness would be inappropriate. A full collar is preferble to a breast collar in the showring as it looks smarter, although correct fit is of much greater importance.

The old rule of black harness with a painted vehicle and brown or russet harness with a varnished wood vehicle is still observed in the showring, although not so rigidly as it once was, and black harness and varnished vehicles are now often seen in combination. Brown harness with a painted vehicle, however, can look ill-matched and distract from the overall appearance of the turnout. While brass

fittings are preferable to nickel in a private driving class, it is more important that the fittings on the harness match the fittings on the vehicle, including the lamps.

The vehicle must be sound and road-worthy and turned out to a high standard in terms of condition of paintwork and upholstery as well as cleanliness. In addition to being the correct fit for the horse, it must be of a suitable type and 'put to' correctly. Pneumatic-tyred vehicles, exercise carts and wire-wheeled show wagons are debarred from private driving classes although some driving shows do include a special class for exercise carts in order to cater for people who do not possess a show vehicle.

The lamps should be of a size and style to match the vehicle and, if the candles are new, they should be lit then blown out, as a candle that has already been lit will light more readily and save time, and everything in a driving class is based on practicality and tradition. A wicker or leather umbrella basket may be attached to the rear of the vehicle but, if one is carried, there should be an umbrella in it. Driving umbrellas are large and sombre-coloured with a brass ring in the centre so that they can be hung from a hook in the coach-house ceiling in the open position to allow the silk covering to dry after use. Modern garishly coloured or striped nylon umbrellas should not be used as they would be out of keeping with the rest of the turnout. 'Spares' should be carried at all times in case of breakages or accidents.

## Correct dress

The dress of the driver or *whip* is very important. A gentleman should wear a suit, soft leather or dogskin gloves, which fit fairly loosely as tight gloves can restrict the movement of the hand, and a bowler hat of a colour to match the wearer's suit. A top hat is generally worn only when driving a tandem or four-in-hand, or on very formal occasions. A small, discreet buttonhole in the lapel is acceptable.

For lady *whips*, a conservatively-coloured outfit, gloves and a narrow-brimmed hat are most suitable. Enormous floppy hats, tight skirts, high-heeled shoes or flamboyant colours should be avoided as practicality must dictate dress, and the wearer should not distract the judge's attention from the rest of the turnout but should blend in and be a part of it. In wet weather, wool or string gloves give a better grip on damp, slippery reins, and a pair can always be carried either in the spares box or under the seat cushion. A whip must always be carried, and a knee rug or apron should be worn to keep the clothes clean as well as the wearer warm and dry in cold or wet weather. If the apron is of a lightweight summer type and liable to flap about at the lower corners, sewing tiny lead weights, such as lead-shot, into pockets in the bottom hem will keep it in place.

Male grooms should dress similarly to the driver in a suit, gloves and bowler, whereas for female grooms riding clothes are suitable and look smart. As the purpose of a groom is to assist generally, when the horse is standing in the line-up at a show it is customary for the groom to get down and stand about 1 m (3 ft) in front of and facing the horse, ready to help if required.

Grooms do not salute or remove their hats except on very formal occasions. If a passenger is being carried, they should never need to get down to help with the horses or any other part of the turnout, but they should salute the judge at the same time as the driver **(Fig. 34)** by bowing their heads, male passengers having first removed their hats. Ladies hold their whips as in **(Fig. 34)**.

Fig. 34 Saluting the judge – **a** lady whip, **b** gentleman whip

## Judging criteria

The classification for private driving classes varies from show to show (although the judging criteria remain the same) and will read as follows:

Horses or ponies, any height, non-Hackney type, four years old or over, to be driven single, pair or tandem to a suitable vehicle. Trade vehicles debarred. A road marathon of approximately four miles will be included.

At some shows where there are likely to be sufficient entries, the class may be subdivided into singles and pairs or tandems, while at the larger driving shows there may be classes for different heights of animals, novice horses or ponies, mountain and moorland ponies, junior whips, and so forth. Sometimes, but not always, a road marathon of a few miles is included so that the judge can see how the horses go on the open road and in traffic as well as in the confines of the showring.

A collecting ring steward will usher exhibitors into the ring when the judge is ready, and the ring steward will advise them what is required. Generally, all the turnouts will be asked to trot around the ring in a clockwise direction, and it is important for an exhibitor to allow plenty of room between their turnout and those both in front and behind so that the judge can see them properly. Avoid getting grouped with other turnouts or behind a horse which is slow moving or which looks likely to misbehave and, if necessary, overtake the turnout in front but always on the inside and with plenty of room in between. The aim of each exhibitor should be to enable the judge to see their horse to best advantage and this will not be possible if others are blocking the judge's view or impeding their horse's progress.

After a few circuits of the ring, the judge may request the stewart to ask exhibitors to 'change rein' or go the other way around the ring so that he or she can see if the horses go equally well both ways. Many horses are one-sided and perform much better on a particular rein. To change direction, cut diagonally across the ring taking care not to interfere with the path of other exhibitors and avoiding any obstacles, such as show jumps. When the judge has seen all competitors equally, the ring steward will call them into line so that the judge can inspect them individually before asking each one to give a brief 'show' to demonstrate the horses obedience, manners and way of going. This usually comprises walking out of line away from the judge so that the horse's response to the aids and straightness of action can be observed, trotting a large figure of eight to assess manners and paces, perhaps an extended trot in a straight line in front of the judge if there is room to show that the horse is capable of changes of pace and that his transitions are crisp and spontaneous, a halt, and a rein-back. The rein-back should be no more than about four paces after which the horse should be walked forward a few strides and halted while the driver salutes the judge by placing the reins and whip in the left hand and removing his hat with the right hand and bowing. A lady *whip* should place the reins in the left hand and bow the head briefly while the right arm raises the whip into a horizontal position so that the elbow is tipped upwards. The horse can then be returned to its former position in the line-up.

When the judge has watched all the individual shows, the ring steward will ask all exhibitors to trot on around the ring while the judge makes his final assessment before instructing the steward to call them back into line in the order of placing. Keep an eye on the steward all the time, and on being called in it is courtesy to acknowledge the steward with a brief salute. Sometimes the judge will drive some of the exhibits to see how they handle before making a final decision.

As the judge in a private driving class will be looking for a forward-going and free-moving horse with impeccable manners, which is a pleasure to drive, any problems encountered, such as pulling, should be concealed from the judge as far as possible. The driver must appear relaxed and confident and in complete control at all times. Where there is a road marathon, maintain an even road pace of around 11 kph (7 mph), and remember to give clear and correct hand signals when slowing down or turning.

When judging a pair turnout, in addition to the other criteria, the judge will be looking for horses that are well matched in size, colour and type and that go well together as a pair, with even paces. He or she will quickly notice if one horse is not doing his share of the work or is pulling excessively or resisting.

Private driving classes are often referred to as pleasure classes in American show schedules, and entries are judged on the suitability of the horse or pony to provide a pleasant drive. Exhibits are usually required to be shown in the ring on both reins and at a walk, collected trot, working trot and 'trot on' or extended trot.

They must stand quietly when asked, and rein-back, and those chosen to do an individual show or 'workout' may be asked to work both ways of the ring at any pace requested by the judge. A figure of eight is generally included. Under the American system of judging on a points basis, performance, manners and way of going account for 70 per cent of the marks; with condition, fit and appropriateness of harness and vehicle 20 per cent; and the attire of the driver 10 per cent.

## Other Types of Showring Classes

### Ride and drive classes

Ride and drive classes provide an opportunity for the versatility of the horse to be demonstrated, and they generally take one or other of two forms of competition.

The first is a speed competition in which each exhibitor drives a set course of obstacle cones, unharnesses, saddles up and rides the horse over a course of small jumps before harnessing up again to drive the cone course a second time. Each competitor is timed and the fastest wins.

The second form of competition is based on style and is not timed. Competitors are all judged together as a private driving class then they leave the ring and return under saddle to be judged as a riding horse class with perhaps one or more optional jumps. Marks are usually awarded 50 per cent in harness and 50 per cent under saddle.

### Obstacle and scurry driving

Obstacle driving classes **(42)** consist of a course of pairs of driving cones set at a measured distance apart and usually incorporating a change of rein, a slalom, and perhaps a U-shaped box of cones, and the winner of the class is the one who completes the course in the fastest time. A penalty of five or perhaps ten seconds, depending on the rules for the classes, is added to the overall time for each ball dislodged from the top of a cone, and any errors-of-course result in elimination from the competition.

42   A competitor in a novelty obstacle driving competition takes exception to crossing an artificial zebra crossing and jumps it instead. The vehicle is a governess car

*Fig. 35* Scurry driving – pairs of ponies negotiate a course of tight turns through 'gates' of cones as fast as possible

A type of obstacle driving is scurry driving, in which pairs of ponies harnessed to special lightweight vehicles with a full front wheel lock and low centre of gravity are driven at speed against the clock around a very tight course **(Fig. 35)**.

A variation of obstacle driving is a 'gambler's stakes' class where each competitor has the same amount of time, usually two minutes, to negotiate as many obstacles as possible. There are between eight and 12 obstacles in the ring, each of which is given a score value according to its degree of difficulty, and drivers try to accrue as many points as possible in the time allowed. Usually, obstacles may be driven in any order and may be approached from either direction. Each obstacle may be attempted twice, but competitors must attempt a different obstacle before returning for a second try. A signal will sound at the end of the time allowed after which the competitor must exit through the finish line. At that point the total time on the course will be recorded and, in the event of equality of points, the fastest time recorded determines the winner.

## Reinsmanship classes

Reinsmanship classes are often included in American driving show schedules and entries are judged, rather like junior *whip* classes are in Britain, primarily on the skill and ability of the driver. Marks are usually awarded, 70 per cent for handling of the reins and whip, control of the horse(s), posture and overall appearance of the driver, and 30 per cent for condition, fit and appropriateness of harness, vehicle and attire.

## *Concours d'élégance*

Concours d'élégance classes are now included at many shows: they are popular with both competitors and spectators. The standard criteria by which private driving classes are judged do not apply, and the *concours d'élégance* is usually judged by an artist, who selects the winners from those turnouts considered to be the most elegant. Judging is done from a distance and the turnouts are not inspected closely as in other show classes. The horse, harness, vehicle, driver and passengers are all taken into account, although the overall elegance of the entire turnout counts more than anything. Fancy dress or period costume is usually debarred, and the performance of the horse(s) is not considered except that a disobedient horse may render the turnout inelegant.

## Fine harness and roadster classes

Fine harness classes are virtually exclusive to America, and the quality and performance of the horse is paramount, with the vehicle and harness being the means of showing it off more than an integral part of the turnout to be judged. The horses are required to show great presence and action and are driven to lightweight four-wheeled fine harness buggies, which are not dissimilar to the show wagons and viceroys in which Hackneys are shown. Most fine harness horses are American Saddlebreds although Morgans are also shown in this style.

Roadster classes are another almost exclusively American type of driving class, and the horses, generally Standardbreds, are driven to lightweight buggies or sulky-type two-wheelers called bikes. The drivers wear 'silks' like racing jockeys and the horses are judged on their paces, which must include a very fast trot. Even in small arenas, it is amazing the speeds these horses can reach.

## *Combined Driving*

Combined driving is now tremendously popular on both sides of the Atlantic and it is based on the ridden three-day event, with three quite separate phases: dressage (including presentation), a cross-country marathon, and obstacle cones. The scores for each phase are collated to give an overall result.

## Presentation and dressage

The purpose of presentation is to judge the condition, cleanliness and safety of the harness and vehicle, the turnout of the horse, and the position and dress of the driver as well as the attire and performance of the groom. Normally, presentation is judged in the collecting ring or at a designated point nearby prior to the dressage tests, but at some smaller events, particularly local club one-day events, presentation may be judged 'on the move' while the competitor is performing his or her dressage test. In such cases, marks are awarded for general impression only. The dressage phase is intended to demonstrate the freedom, regularity and distinction of paces, and the harmony, impulsion, suppleness and obedience of the horse(s) on the move. The test is driven in a measured arena, 100 m by 40 m for singles or pairs, and the competitor will be assessed on his or her style of driving, accuracy, and general command of the horse(s) **(Fig. 36)**. The actual dressage test consists of a prescribed series of movements involving changes of pace and direction, and marks are awarded from 0–10 for each individual movement as well as for paces, impulsion, obedience and driver. Each test is judged by two judges, one of whom is positioned at the top of the arena with the other seated half-way along one side of the arena so that the straightness and accuracy of each movement can be fairly assessed. The total marks awarded by each judge are added together and divided by two then deducted from the maximum possible to give a penalty score. The competitor with the lowest penalty score will be placed highest in the dressage phase.

● **_Walk_** A regular four-beat rhythm, moving freely forward and covering the ground, the horse maintaining a light even contact with the reins.

● **_Working trot_** An active, well-balanced two-beat rhythm with the head carried more elevated than at the walk.

● **_Collected trot_** A shorter-striding, more animated pace without loss of impulsion or cadence with the head carried higher and the neck showing more flexion at the poll.

● **_Extended trot_** The hind legs well engaged to propel the horse forward with longer strides and less collection.

● **_Rein-back_** Although not classed as a pace as such, the rein-back is a two-beat rhythm and it should be straight, even and unrushed.

When driving a dressage test, use the arena fully by keeping close to the boards that mark the perimeter, and make sure that transitions are made promptly at the appropriately lettered marker and that the paces are clearly defined. Even if the horse is unable to show much variation of pace in the trot, emphasize the transition by, for example, slowing pace a little before going into an extended trot so that the judge is made aware of the change of pace, and aim for rhythm and fluency at all times.

Figures should be well-rounded and even. In the case of 20 m circles, if they are to be executed down the long sides of the arena, by making sure the inner part of the movement is either on X or on the centre track marked by previous competitors the correct circumference of the circle will be guaranteed. Spacial awareness of the size of the arena is a great help in assessing the

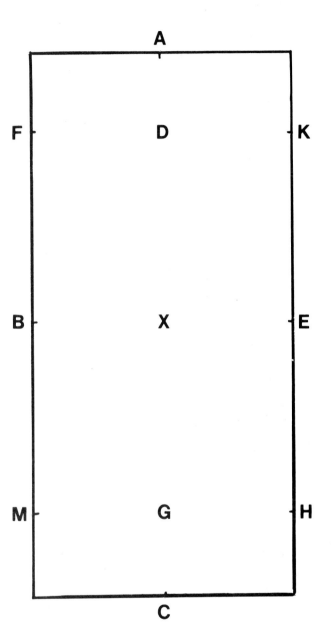

_Fig. 36_ Dressage arena (40 × 100m)

correct measurements of individual movements, and a practice arena of the proper dimensions at home is invaluable. If an error-of-course is made, a bell will be sounded and the competitor should go back to the beginning of the movement.

When learning a dressage test prior to an event, it is always helpful to draw each movement on a piece of paper marked out with the letters of the arena, remembering that it is easy to get confused or even lost when looking down the arena from the opposite end so do not make the mistake of learning the test from one angle only. 'Walking' the whole test on foot using a rectangular shape like a rug for the arena can assist those who find learning a test difficult. Avoid practising the test too often with the horse and vehicle as a clever horse will soon memorise parts of the test and anticipate the movements, spoiling the overall effect.

## Cross-country marathon

The heart of a combined driving event is the cross-country, and the purpose of this phase is to test the fitness and stamina of the horse and the skill and horsemanship of the competitor. The course is divided into a number of sections, usually five, with the second and fourth sections at a walk and the other three at a trot although at local club events or at one-day events the cross-country or marathon phase is often limited to three sections, one of which is a walk section. Novice classes at larger events may be similarly restricted in length.

A 'time allowed' is calculated for each section and penalties are accrued for either exceeding this or for finishing a particular section before the minimum time. Further penalties may be accrued for breaking from the pace specified for the section by walking or cantering in the trot section to lose or make up time or by trotting in the walk

section. Penalties are also added for halts other than for an accident or hold-up on the course, or for errors-of-course due to missing a marker flag. In all but the walk sections, natural hazards like steep gradients are included, and in section C there are a number of artificial hazards to be negotiated. Each hazard is surrounded by a 20 m penalty area marked out with a line of sawdust, and the route or routes, as there may be a choice to be taken through the hazards, is marked out with red and white flags and lettered markers, which must be followed in alphabetical sequence keeping the red flags on the right and the white flags on the left.

Penalties are picked up for exceeding the time allowed for each individual hazard, turning the vehicle over, the driver or groom(s) dismounting, the driver putting down his whip, disconnecting the traces, or any part of the turnout leaving the penalty area before completing the hazard. The total penalties for the marathon are calculated to determine the placings for that section of the event. The rules and regulations governing combined driving are subject to frequent review and amendments, and it is important to read the rule book and to be conversant with it before entering an event as contravening the rules could lead to elimination.

## Obstacle driving phase

The final section of a combined driving event is the obstacle driving, and the aim is to test the fitness, obedience and suppleness of the horse after the marathon and the skill of the driver at precision driving. Each competitor must drive a course of about 20 pairs of obstacle cones within a

**43** Miss Jane Brindley driving her Fell pony gelding Edenview Moonstroller through the watersplash hazard on the marathon phase of a combined driving event

specified time allowed, and penalty marks are incurred for knocking over a cone or displacing the ball from the top, exceeding the time allowed, errors-of-course, or putting a groom down. To make the course more interesting, multiple obstacles may be included as well as a watersplash, a wooden bridge to be driven over, or obstacles made of straw bales or show jump wings and poles. The section is judged by either accrued penalty marks for displacing obstacles or exceeding the time limit being added to the overall score, or by counting penalties as seconds and adding them to the competitor's time for the course, with the fastest time winning.

The total marks for each section of the event are added together to determine the final placings. As combined driving is a very demanding sport, the horse(s) needs to be extremely fit, which means many months of preparation and schooling prior to an event, and the harness and vehicle used need to be very strong and capable of withstanding a lot of strain, especially during the marathon phase. A short compulsory halt is included at the end of the two walk sections of a full marathon and if a horse appears to be exhausted, in distress or lame, the event officials can demand its withdrawal from the event, so it is pointless as well as potentially cruel to enter a horse for a combined driving event before it is ready.

## Transporting a Driving Turnout

Competing at any level will invariably involve transporting the driving turnout and there are a number of ways of going about this. The ideal method is to use a motorized horsebox into which both the vehicle and horse(s) can be loaded. An electric or hand-operated winch with the cable fastened around the axle of the vehicle will make loading the vehicle a relatively easy operation. It is advisable to load the vehicle before the horse(s) so that in the event of an accident or emergency the horses can be unloaded quickly without the vehicle being in the way although a side ramp on the horsebox may preclude this problem. Even with a small horsebox, if the vehicle is a two-wheeler and is loaded in backwards with the shafts fastened to the roof and pointing towards the rear there will probably be sufficient room to travel at least one horse in comfort under the shafts. The wheels must be securely chocked to prevent them moving, and the shafts, wheels, springs or steps firmly tied using soft rags under the ropes to avoid damage to the paintwork. A lightweight dust-sheet tied over the vehicle will help to keep it clean while in transit. A strong partition between the vehicle and horses is essential, and make sure that the horses are tied up in such a way that they cannot reach any part of the vehicle to chew it or rub themselves on it.

The seat cushions are removed from the vehicle and carried separately, and the lamps transported in a wooden box well wrapped in soft rags. Canvas sleeves lined in foam rubber can also be used to protect lamps from damage. The whip should be carried on a flat whip-board incorporating a reel at the top to maintain the shape of the thong. Harness should ideally be transported in a strong wooden harness chest. By wrapping each part of the harness in thick, soft cloths, damage to patent leather facings will be prevented.

Some competitors transport their vehicle on a flat-bed trailer towed either behind a wagon or a car. Although loading onto a low trailer may be easier than into a wagon, the vehicle is likely to get dirty in transit from dust or mud thrown up off the road, and even a waterproof tarpaulin cover does not eliminate the problem entirely.

For those people who do not possess a wagon and do not want the trouble and expense of taking two cars, one to tow the vehicle on a flat-trailer and the other to tow the horse in a horse-trailer, there are two alternatives. The first is to use one of the extra large horse-trailers especially designed for driving horses, which have enough room to accommodate both the vehicle and up to two horses. Apart from being very expensive, these trailers are heavy and require a substantial towing vehicle and even then their excessive loaded weight can make them a liability on steep hills or in strong winds. A better proposition is to use a pickup truck onto which the vehicle can be loaded using ramps and a winch, and the horses can be towed behind in a normal horse trailer. The ability to transport the whole turnout together far outweighs the disadvantages of having to unhitch the trailer to unload the vehicle or the fact that the vehicle is open to the weather and in an exposed position despite the use of protective covers. As space will be at a premium with a pickup and trailer, a waterproof metal trunk secured in the back under the vehicle can be useful for carrying harness, lamps and so forth, and the whip-board will usually fit at the back of the cab behind the seats.

### Competing checklist

A checklist of things needed at a show or event and pinned up at home can be invaluable and save the frustration of finding on show-day that something essential has been left at home. Everything, from the harness, lamps, apron and whip down to an anti-sweat rug, grooming kit, wet-weather wear and purple antiseptic spray in case of minor injuries, should be listed and ticked off as it is loaded.

## Be Self-Critical

Competing entails a great deal of hard work and dedication, but success also involves an element of realistic self-criticism because only if you are aware of weak areas can you expect to improve. Most judges will give constructive advice if politely asked after the show and, although the subjective views of individual judges are likely to differ to a degree, there will be some common ground which can be built into future training programmes. Above all, competing should be fun and the will to succeed should not distract from the pleasure of driving horses as a sport.

---

### SUMMARY

**When competing with a driving turnout:**
- Never take a young or inexperienced horse to a show or event without getting him used to the company of other turnouts first
- In the showring never drive too close to the carriage in front or overtake at speed
- Remember to signal to other drivers before stopping or turning
- Never allow a horse to canter or gallop in harness
- Never use a new vehicle or harness for the first time at a show
- Never leave a horse tied to a wagon or trailer when still harnessed to a vehicle

**Remember to take:**
- Lamps
- Apron
- Whip
- Exhibitors badges/car passes
- Spares
- Grooming kit/polishing cloths for the vehicle
- Haynet and water bucket
- Anti-sweat rug
- Spare set of clothes

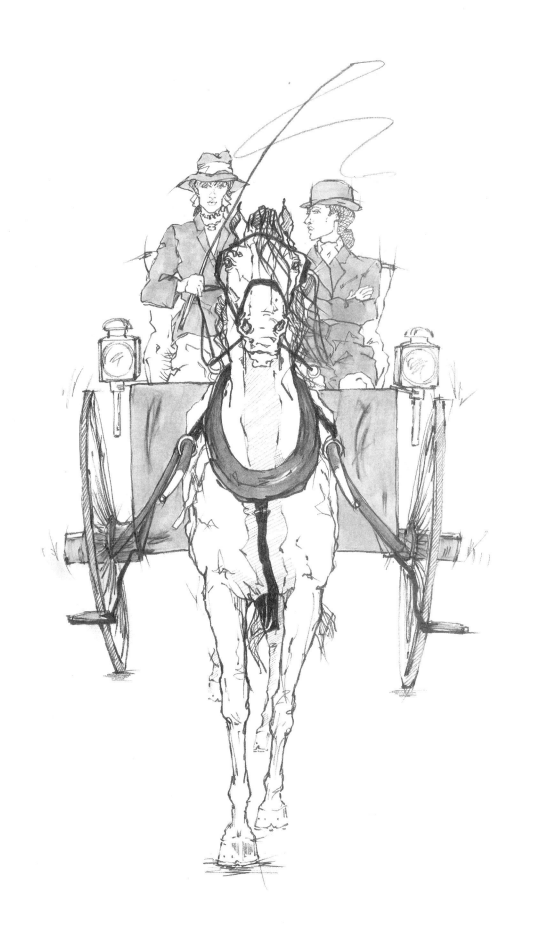

## Part 3
# KEEPING GOING

# 8
# RESTORATION OF VEHICLES

## Home Restoration Techniques

For many people new to driving, finding and restoring an old and perhaps dilapidated vehicle to make it roadworthy and smart, then having the satisfaction of driving it at rallies and shows, adds a new dimension to their involvement in the sport. Apart from the challenge and interest of do-it-yourself restoration, it can be an inexpensive way of acquiring an antique vehicle in show-ring condition with the added benefit of knowing exactly what is beneath the paintwork and how sound the vehicle is. Unrestored vehicles, varying from examples requiring total rebuilding to others just in need of repainting, can usually be picked up at the collective carriage sales now regularly organized in different parts of the country, and individual vehicles sometimes turn up unexpectedly at farm and country house sales as well as at horse sales and through newspaper advertisements.

Unless the buyer is exceptionally skilled in woodworking techniques, vehicles requiring more than minor structural repairs should be left for professional restorers as the cost of a wheelwright's services could suddenly turn what seemed a bargain into a prohibitively expensive project. A thorough examination of the vehicle should be made prior to purchase to assess the work required to restore it in terms of materials, time and skill levels as well as to ensure it is the right size and that all other essential criteria are met.

### Dismantling and labelling

The first stage of any restoration work is to dismantle the vehicle completely, taking care to label every part down to the last nut and bolt so that after restoration the vehicle can be reassembled as before. By ensuring that every part is replaced exactly as it was, using the same screws and bolts, a good fit is guaranteed and the originality of the vehicle is maintained. Using polythene bags to hold small parts like shaft fittings together with their screws is a good idea as the bag can be fastened and labelled to show the contents and which side of the vehicle they came off. Larger parts like steps should have their fastening bolts kept together in a bag tied to the part to prevent them being lost. The liberal use of penetrating oil or lubricating sprays will help to loosen parts that have not moved for years, and paint remover and a wire brush may be needed on nuts and bolts that are clogged up under layers of old paint. Using force should be avoided as apart from damaging the thread of bolts or even shearing them

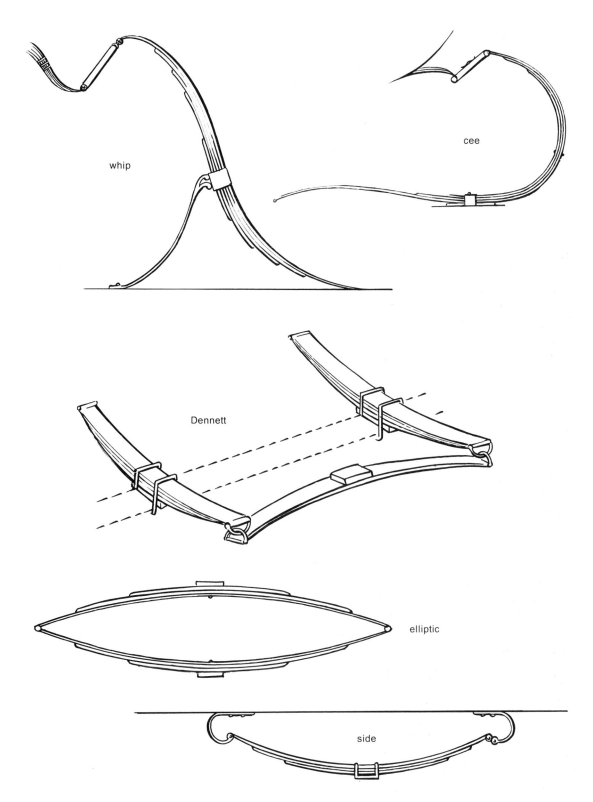

whip

cee

Dennett

elliptic

side

*Fig. 37* Types of springs

off, the pressure exerted may cause cracks in the surrounding woodwork. Any broken or badly worn parts should be noted and put to one side for repair or replacement as necessary. The leaves of the springs **(Fig. 37)** will be held together by a single bolt usually in the centre, and caution should be taken unscrewing the nut as the pressure from the leaves will cause it to fly off when released. A useful idea is to tie a rope around the middle of the spring using a slip knot, which will hold the leaves together until the bolt is removed, after which the rope can be gradually loosened to free the leaves. Another method is to grip the whole spring in a large strong vice until the bolt is removed.

### Rusted or corroded ironwork

All painted metal parts including springs, steps, lamp brackets and so forth are likely to be badly rusted and will need to be stripped down completely. As it is difficult to do this effectively and thoroughly at home, it is best to send all the parts away to a specialist firm to be shot-blasted. Badly corroded and pitted ironwork, particularly leaf springs, may be too badly rusted for restoration in which case replacements will be necessary. Commercial motor spring manufacturers will often oblige by copying original springs as a one-off order, and it is a good idea to get a couple of extra spring leaves made at the same time to have put away in case of breakages. Very worn springs will be too 'soft' and bouncy, and the extra pressure put on the individual leaves by the increased movement may cause old and brittle leaves to snap. A breaking spring leaf makes a loud crack like a gun going off and is likely to startle the most docile of horses. Replacement parts should match the original in material and design to maintain the authenticity of the vehicle.

After shot-blasting, the metal parts should be zinc-painted to discourage them from rusting again, and many firms that undertake shot-blasting work also have a facility to dip or spray metal parts with zinc or some other form of anti-rust coating. Some vehicles have decorative metal beading along the sides and top of the body, and rubbing it with abrasive liquid and an old rag will usually reveal it to be brass.

### Woodworm, rot and accidental damage

All the woodwork should be carefully examined for signs of rot, woodworm or accidental damage, and any seriously defective areas replaced using the same type of wood as the original if possible. Sometimes a skilled joiner will make individual replacement parts like mudguards, a dashboard or even side panels provided he is given detailed plans and perhaps what is left of the original as a guide.

Well-seasoned wood should always be used or the new part may well warp in time, putting the vehicle body out of alignment. Unless woodworm damage is severe, the area can be treated with a brush-on insecticide and the tiny holes filled with a fibreglass or plastic wood filler of which there are now innumerable types available on the market. If new wood is used in an original vehicle, it will probably be necessary to paint the vehicle as, under a coat of varnish only, the new wood would clearly show and spoil the overall appearance of the carriage.

Although it is possible to repair broken or cracked shafts using metal plates, it is often easier and safer to replace both shafts with new ones of similar size and shape. In such cases, the original shaft furnishing like tug stops should be used on the new shafts if possible.

## Wheels and axles

Usually if a vehicle has stood neglected for years, the wheels will have suffered most and it is well worth the expense of getting a knowledgable wheelwright to check the wheels and make good any defective parts. Frequently, only the felloes nearest the ground when the vehicle was stored need replacement. Cracks in the hub should be referred to a wheelwright as should loose spokes, although if the vehicle was stored in a very dry place a good soak in a trough of water may swell the wood and tighten up the spokes. As the wheels take so much strain, it is worth seeking professional advice if you are doubtful about any parts. Sometimes, faults in the woodwork are concealed by the old paint and it is not until the vehicle is stripped down that they become apparent. Badly worn or loose tyres can be replaced by the wheelwright, who will also re-channel the wheels if necessary.

When removing the wheels, it is important to keep the wheel nuts and collets together in labelled bags, although some carriage builders stamped the nuts and collets with either R or L to denote whether they went on the right or left side. The brass hub caps, which are often engraved or stamped with the carriage builder's name, should be removed with a proper trap spanner or an adjustable spanner. A hammer and chisel should never be used as it cuts into the soft brass and disfigures the hub cap. Old, dried-on axle grease should be scraped off with a blunt knife, then the axle tree washed off with petrol to clean it. Often the name of the firm who manufactured the ironwork for the carriage builder will be engraved on the axle along with the date of manu-

44 Mrs Mary Nygaard driving a Morgan horse to an American phaeton

facture on the underside. The axle trees should be smeared with fresh grease and wrapped in oily cloth to prevent them rusting while the wheels are off, and the axle itself should be rubbed down using a wire brush and coarse sandpaper then zinc-painted once the surface is smooth.

## Leather dashboards and mudguards

On some vehicles, particularly gigs, the dashboard and mudguards are often leather covered and it is likely that the leather will have perished or rotted away as the metal frames underneath rusted. If so, the remaining leather should be removed and the frames sent away for shot-blasting and zinc-painting after which they can be top-coated in black before being sent to a reputable saddler to be recovered. While it is possible to do the job at home, it is difficult to get the leather pulled tautly over the frame and stitched evenly and neatly, and a saddler will be able to do it more easily. Plain black leather can be used but patent leather looks better for vehicles that will be used for showing, although it scratches easily and needs to be treated with care.

Sometimes the original leather on the dashboard and mudguards is sound and intact, but the surface is lumpy and hard because the japanning on the patent leather has dried out and formed resinous lumps. Attempts to remove the old japanning with chemical solvents are rarely successful, and the leather usually has to be removed. A saddler will also be able to fit new leather on the shaft ends and under the breeching dees. This job can be done at home by carefully removing what is left of the old leather and using it as a pattern to cut new pieces. These are then secured in place with glue to prevent them wrinkling or creasing, and with the edges stitched together on the underside using two needles and two lengths of cat-gut or waxed thread in a cross-over pattern. If the leather is not patent it can be soaked in water first so that it shrinks after being fitted as it dries out and grips more tightly, and the edges of the leather can be folded under for a neater appearance.

Leather hoods often crack and perish along the creases if the hood has been left folded when the vehicle was in storage but, as hoods are expensive to have recovered by a saddler, it may be worth trying to renovate the original leather. Harness oil or liquid leather restorer should be liberally applied to the whole hood and the leather gently manipulated, especially along the folds, to work the oil in and help restore its suppleness. Only when the leather is pliable again should the hood be fully raised as this stretches the leather on the framework and could cause a dried-out and brittle hood to crack or even tear. The lining of the hood is almost certain to need renewing, but a saddler or upholsterer should be able to oblige, using a material of the same colour and type as the seat cushions to maintain uniformity.

## Stripping old paintwork

The most arduous part of the restoration process is removing all the old paint and varnish down to the bare wood. Liquid paint stripper and a blunt paint scraper are the best tools for this job, but care must be taken to ensure that over-enthusiastic scraping does not leave score marks, which are difficult to disguise later, on the wood. Also, some acid paint strippers are inclined to bleach certain types of wood, which would not matter if the vehicle were to be repainted but might be a problem if the intention were to leave the vehicle with a natural wood finish. A small brush with stiff bristles can be useful for removing softened paint from around the base of spokes, or a wire brush gently used can be very effective. With areas of thick, hardened paint, several applications of paint stripper followed by vigorous scraping may be needed to get down to the bare wood. Blow lamps can be used for paint removal but unless handled with skill can leave scorch marks in the wood. The process frequently reveals the various colour schemes the vehicle has had over the years, including the original paintwork and lining, and some restorers like to revert to the vehicle's original colours when choosing paints and upholstery.

Once the bulk of the paint has been removed, all the woodwork should be thoroughly sandpapered to remove the last vestiges of paint. 'Wet and dry' paper is particularly effective. Electric sanders can only be used on flat areas of woodwork and, unless carefully used, they can leave lines and ridges in the wood, and sanding discs on power drills in the hands of an amateur can result in crescent-shaped grooves, which are very difficult and time-consuming to fill in. If the vehicle is going to be finished in natural, varnished wood, it is important to get every trace of paint out of the grain of the wood as the varnish will show it up clearly, especially in daylight. At the end of the sandpapering process, all surfaces on the vehicle should be absolutely free of paint and as smooth as glass. Any metal work that cannot be shot-blasted, like the wheel channels and hub collars, should be sanded down using coarse-grain paper followed by 'wet and dry' then zinc-painted. Smaller metal fittings, like spring shackles or tailgate hinges, can be soaked in paint stripper then wire brushed, sanded and zinc-painted, making sure any moving parts are left free.

## Preparing wood surfaces and priming

A liberal coat of clear wood preservative is a good idea on old, dried out wood and the dissembled vehicle should be left in a well-ventilated place to dry thoroughly before the next stage of the process. Using a flexible-bladed putty knife and a good-quality wood filler, any tiny cracks, wood-worm holes or screw holes should be filled. If the wood filler is of the non-shrink variety, there is no need to fill any imperfections so the filler stands proud of the wood, and it is advisable to use a flexible filler which will move with the 'give' of the wood and not come loose. When the filler has dried out completely, the wood should be sanded down again so that the filled areas cannot be discerned.

The aim of the initial coats of paint is to fill the grain of the wood and provide a smooth, even surface for the subsequent coats. Aluminium primer is ideal as it seals the bare wood, and several thin layers should be applied, allowing each layer to dry thoroughly before the next layer is added. Light sanding followed by a wipe with a clean cloth is advisable between each coat. The paint should never be applied thickly as it dries too slowly and the finished result is never as good as when several thin coats are applied. The aluminium primer is followed by the first undercoat, which again must be allowed to dry and harden completely before being lightly sanded down and wiped before the next layer of undercoat is applied. The process is repeated over and over again until any uneven areas have been filled and the whole surface of the vehicle is absolutely smooth. Up to 16 coats of undercoat may be needed to build up sufficient thickness of paint to obtain the required smoothness and only then should preparations be made to apply the top coat.

## Painting and lining

Professional coachpainters at one time never used gloss paint at all but obtained the final finish with several coats of varnish over matt paint. These days, as matt paint in appropriate colours can be as difficult to obtain as heavy-quality clear varnishes which will not discolour or yellow with age, gloss paint is widely used. A warm, dry, dust-free room is essential for applying the top coats and, as the vehicle will be in parts, it may be possible to bring it indoors and use a spare room as a temporary paint shop. If the room is not centrally heated, an electric fire or portable gas heater could be used to raise the temperature and hasten the drying time of the paint.

If a garage or outdoor workshop has to be used, the floor should be swept meticulously and dampened to lay any dust the day before painting commences, and rags should be pushed under the door and around the windows to prevent draughts, which could stir up any residual dust. Using large sheets of polythene to make a

**45** Mr C. Richardson driving his Fell pony mare, Border Black Empress, to a cee-spring wicker gig. As well as being very lightweight, wickerwork is surprisingly strong and does not show everyday wear and tear as readily as paintwork

dust-free painting booth which can be inexpensively heated can be a good idea and, if there is still any dust in the air, the use of a fine mist spray several hours before painting begins will settle it. Damp or very cold atmospheric conditions can affect the paint and result in a dull or opaque finish. The gloss paint should be applied thinly and evenly and left to dry completely before being rubbed down lightly with fine glass paper. As many coats of gloss paint should be applied as necessary to obtain the required finish and depth of colour.

Although purists may not agree, very acceptable results can be obtained by spray painting a vehicle with cellulose automobile paint. No undercoating is necessary provided the surface is very smooth and, although the paint is designed for metal car bodies, it does not crack even with the slight flexibility of wood. It is also durable and hard, relatively inexpensive considering that no undercoat has to be purchased, and spray painting saves a lot of time.

Whatever type of paint is used, it is useful to order a little extra paint which can be put away and used later for touching up scratches or chips or for painting replacement parts like shafts. Matching paint can be very difficult as even basic colours can vary between paint manufacturers, and most paints darken slightly as they dry, and a tin of touch-up paint can save much frustration later on.

Lining out the wheels, shafts and springs is a skilled job requiring great patience and a steady hand. Special brushes called lining pencils **(Fig. 38)** are used. They have short, wooden handles and long bristles, which help to keep the line straight as well as acting as a good reservoir for the paint. Confidence and boldness are needed to line successfully with brushes as the faster the paint is applied the straighter the lines are likely to be. Quite satisfactory results can be obtained with patent lining devices, which resemble large fountain pens with revolving paint wheels at the end instead of nibs. To do the line around the wheel felloes, it is easiest to spin the wheel on a special stand or on the axle and apply the brush to the felloe as it revolves, holding the thumb against the channel to keep the line evenly spaced in the middle of the felloe. Attention needs to be paid to ensure that the ends of the line match up perfectly. Lining in the form of rolls of fine adhesive strips is now obtainable, but it looks unprofessional and is inclined to lift off the paintwork in time. Generally, lines are only painted on the outer felloes, spokes and hubs of the wheels, on the springs and on the upper and outer sides of the shafts. Garish or excessive lining should be avoided. Finally, one or more coats of clear varnish should be applied to protect the paintwork and improve the depth of gloss of the paint, then the vehicle can be reassembled.

Spring shackles, bolt heads and nuts should be gloss-painted and given time to dry thoroughly before assembly, taking care not to get any paint on the threads. A small, rubber-headed hammer can be useful for gently tapping bolts into fittings made tight by new layers of paint but, failing this, a thick cloth bound around the head of an ordinary hammer will serve the same purpose. After assembly, every part should be very carefully checked, especially the fitting of the wheels on the

*Fig. 38* Lining pencil

axle, as if the nuts are too tight, the friction can generate heat, causing the metal to expand and the wheels to seize up on the axle trees. Liberal greasing is essential to ensure that the wheels can rotate freely on the axle, and a light smearing of grease between the individual leaves of the springs will help to keep them free-moving.

The most suitable floor covering is ribbed rubber matting as it gives a good grip for the feet in any weather and can easily be removed and washed down when necessary. Most industrial floor-covering specialists stock it and sell it by the metre or yard off a roll.

**46** Mr and Mrs Mike Kasica's partbred Arab, Galena, driven to an American runabout. Note the transverse elliptic springs and longitudinal perch on the vehicle

## Renewing upholstery

Usually, the upholstery will be rotted away, eaten by mice or infested with moths and beyond redemption, although the original horsehair cushions may be worth salvaging to have recovered and rebuttoned. If new cushions are needed, high density foam is the most satisfactory modern material as it maintains its shape well and is not too soft. Suitable materials for upholstery are hide, good quality leather cloth, Bedford cord, Melton cloth, or any hard-wearing plain fabric. Nylon or other very smooth materials are best avoided because slippery seat cushions could be dangerous if they caused the driver to slide forward and lose his position. A professional upholsterer can usually be persuaded to undertake fitted upholstery work like the buttoned pad-

ding lining the seats of round-backed gigs, and will cover seat cushions and back rests. Buttoned and diamond pleating, staggered buttoning or plain padding are all acceptable upholstery styles depending on the type of vehicle, but a row of brass-headed studs around the edge of any upholstery looks gawdy and over-decorative.

## Restoring carriage lamps

Occasionally a vehicle for restoration is sold with its original lamps, or perhaps lamps are purchased separately, which are suitable for the vehicle but require renovation. If buying lamps to go on a specific vehicle, make sure they are of a size and design in keeping with the vehicle, and check their condition carefully before purchasing. Broken or cracked panes of glass or corroded side panels and stems are a job for a professional antique restorer, although there are now a number of specialist lamp repairers who can also supply parts, such as new stems. Lamps that are basically sound can be restored at home by stripping the lamp down to the bare metal using paint stripper, a stiff brush and sandpaper then priming, under-coating and painting the body. Any brass work, including stems and the metal trim around the panes, should be cleaned with metal polish only. Often the linen-covered spring inside the stem is badly rusted and may need replacing, and there are inevitably heavy deposits of old candle wax clogging the floor of the lamp and the top of the stem. These can be carefully removed with a blunt knife. A few drops of penetrating oil will help free rusted-up door hinges, and the polished interior of the lamp can be cleaned with silver polish.

Proper slow-burning carriage lamp candles are now readily obtainable through specialist harness stores or driving sundries suppliers. When secured in their brackets on the vehicle, the lamps should be well clear of the wheels to allow for the body to dip on the springs without risk of the lamp striking the top of the wheel, and a narrow leather strap slipped through the metal lug on the underside of the lamp body and buckled around the bracket will ensure that the lamp cannot jolt loose when the vehicle is in motion. If the lamp does not fit securely in the bracket, a little piece of leather fastened around the top of the stem will generally make it grip more firmly.

# 9

# CARE AND MAINTENANCE OF EQUIPMENT

## *Storage of Vehicles*

Proper care and maintenance of carriages, harness and ancillary driving equipment substantially increases their working life and prevents them becoming shabby prematurely. Vehicles should be stored in a dry, well-ventilated building with as consistent a temperature as possible, as extremes of heat and cold, dampness or direct sunlight can all crack or discolour the paint or varnish. If the building has windows or roof-lights it is as well to cover them so that the vehicle is stored in perpetual shade, as this eliminates the risk of the paint fading or bubbling, and the building should be away from manure heaps or stables as the ammonia can also damage paintwork. For this reason, it is undesirable to store a horse-drawn vehicle in or near a stable despite the fact that at one time stables and coach-houses were all too frequently combined. A very dry atmosphere should be avoided as it can cause the wood to shrink, resulting in loose spokes or cracked body panels and, if the building is heated and excessively dry, a large bowl of water kept continually near the vehicle can maintain a reasonable humidity level. Two-wheeled vehicles should never be stored with their shafts resting on the ground, which can cause them to warp, but should have them supported on a trestle or shaft stand (**Fig. 39**), and poles should be detached from the vehicle and either laid on a thick cloth under the vehicle, kept on a special rack similar to the type used for the storage of rowing oars or, if the building is high enough, slung from a beam by the pole-end so they hang down. Poles should never be propped up in a corner as this encourages them to warp. If a shaft stand is not available, two-wheelers can be satisfactorily stored by placing a strong length of wood with one end resting on the axle and the other end on the ground behind the vehicle then tipping the vehicle backwards until the body rests on the wood. Tying the shafts to a beam will prevent them falling to the ground if the vehicle is knocked inadvertently. Wheels should be chocked to prevent them moving, and hoods should be left up as closed hoods are liable to crack along the folds.

If the vehicle is to be stored for a long period, the axle(s) should be rested on empty oil drums or something similar so that the wheels are clear of the ground and free to rotate or the wheels may buckle and the rubber tyres flatten where they are in contact with the ground. If it is not possible to lift the vehicle off the ground, it is important regularly to alter the position of the wheels by rotating each one a quarter turn every week, and a dust sheet thrown

Fig. 39 Two-wheeled vehicles should be stored at all times with the shafts supported

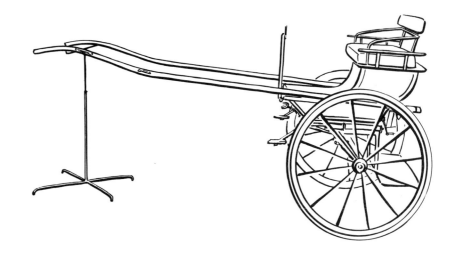

47 Mrs Barbara Kasica driving her part-bred Friesian, Batavier, to a modern Harewood gig, a dual purpose vehicle suitable for both showing and cross-country driving

over the vehicle will help prevent dust and gritty particles harming the paintwork. Fitted shaft, wheel and body covers, which help to protect a vehicle both in storage and in transit, are now commercially available. Cushions can be removed and stored somewhere safe and dry, but fitted upholstery, such as seat backs as well as hood linings are best sprayed with a mild solution of insecticide to discourage moths then, if possible, covered with cloths to keep them clean. Strategically placed moth balls can also effectively discourage insects. Polythene should not be used to cover upholstery as, being non-porous, it can hold in condensation and moisture, causing fustiness.

## Care of Equipment

### Regular maintenance of vehicles

After a vehicle has been used, the lamps and cushions should be removed then the floor mats should be taken out and shaken and the interior swept out. The vehicle can then be washed down using plenty of cold water or the gritty particles will scratch the paintwork. Begin with the wheels, which should be jacked up **(Fig. 40)** to facilitate cleaning between the spokes. A hosepipe only should be used until the bulk of the mud is washed off and, if the jet is of limited force, the loosened mud will not be splashed onto other parts of the vehicle. A very soft sponge will remove any remaining dirt but it must be carefully and gently used or it will scour the paint with the abrasive mud particles left behind. Dried-on horse dung, which is often picked up on showfields, must be soaked off with plenty of water or it can lift the paint off as it is removed. Grease or oil can be sponged off using a little liquid soap on a sponge, and specks of tar are best rubbed off with a little petrol on a rag.

Finally, the whole vehicle should be given a thorough rinse then dried off using a chamois leather. Those vehicles which have been spray-painted with automobile paint can be polished with one of the many patent preparations made specifically for use on cars and which protect the paintwork as well as giving it a deep shine.

Leather parts, including dashboards and mudguards, should be wiped over with a damp cloth and very occasionally given a light oiling; otherwise they should be polished with a good quality leather blacking. Patent leather is best cleaned with a proprietory patent leather cleaner or a little top of the milk applied to the surface and polished off with a soft cloth, and metal fittings can be cleaned with liquid metal polish and burnished with a clean rag. Upholstery can be brushed or vacuumed to remove dust or horse-hair but, if it is wet, it must be allowed to dry thoroughly first. Dirty marks on the surface can usually be sponged out with warm, soapy water. Hide upholstery should be wiped clean and occasionally treated with leather cream to prevent it drying out and cracking.

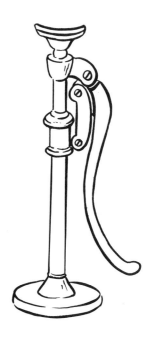

Fig. 40 Jack

Axle trees, particularly those of the mail box type, should be regularly greased, and any grease or oil on the outside of the hub should be wiped off with petrol on a rag. Grease escaping from the inside of the hub of a collinge axle could indicate that the leather washer, the purpose of which is to keep the grease in, is worn and in need of replacement. The turntable or fifth wheel on four-wheelers should also be cleaned periodically with petrol to remove the old grease, which will be gritty and hard, and fresh lubrication should be applied to the plates.

## Care of carriage lamps

Lamps should not be left on vehicles when not in use, but stored separately. Tack rooms at one time were equipped with a wooden shelf in which pairs of holes were cut for the lamp stems to fit into, and this provided a safe and easy system, which is still often copied today. Alternatively, the lamps can be kept in the bottom of a harness cupboard or trunk although it is worth having canvas sleeves lined with foam rubber for the lamps to fit into to avoid scratching them. Custom-built wooden carrying boxes for lamps are ideal and lessen the danger of the glass panes being broken or cracked, especially when being transported to shows. Lamps should always be kept away from heat or direct sunlight, as the candles will melt, and coarse abrasive cleaners should never be used on the silvered interior.

## Restoration of old harness

Harness which is old or which has not been used for some considerable time will have become stiff but liberal applications of neatsfoot oil or some other leather preparation can render it usable again provided the leather is otherwise sound and not cracking, and the buckles have not corroded. A reputable saddler would check a set of harness over, renewing any worn or broken parts, restuffing the pad if necessary, and repairing any rotted stitching.

## Storage of harness

Harness is ideally stored on special racks in a glass-fronted harness case but, failing that, it can be hung on the walls of a tack room or laid carefully in a chest of deep drawers or in an wooden harness chest. If harness is hung up, hooks or nails must not be used as the weight of the harness will be concentrated on one place, causing the leather to crack or stretch under the strain. Wooden or metal harness brackets should be used, preferably covered in felt or foam rubber to protect the leather, or large turned wooden bobbins or even old tins nailed to the wall can be used to support the bridle, the collar and traces, the reins, and the pad complete with backstrap, crupper and breeching. A dry dust-free but airy place is required for storing harness as in damp conditions mould and mildew can attack the leather while the humidity causes metalwork to rust. Extremely dry conditions will result in the leather drying out and becoming brittle, and extremes in temperature are especially bad for patent leather, the surface of which can become textured, covered in tiny cracks, or milky in appearance. Patent leather also marks easily, with the impression of whatever has been laid alongside or on top of it, and each part of the harness should be wrapped individually in thick smooth cloth to avoid being damaged. Even coarse woven materials like hessian can mark patent leather, particularly in warm conditions when the lacquered surface of the leather will be more pliable. A few mothballs in the harness cupboard or chest will keep insects at bay.

48  Mr A. Rosenburg driving his Canadian part-breds, King George and Prince Tom, to a slat-sided phaeton at the Myopia driving event in Massachusetts

## Maintenance of harness

After use, harness should be taken apart and wiped over with a damp cloth to remove sweat, mud and grease. In order to keep it supple, the leather should be lightly oiled using a compound like neats-foot oil at regular intervals although only as much oil as the leather will absorb should be applied or the surface will become too greasy to polish. Wax-type shoe polish sparingly applied to the outer surface only and vigorously brushed and polished with a soft cloth will give a good top shine. Driving reins should be oiled occasionally, and at all other times cleaned with glycerine saddle soap, which softens and preserves the leather. Patent leather can again be cleaned with either a proprietory dressing or the top of the milk, and the metal fittings with liquid metal polish. Pieces of leather or stiff card, with a slit cut in them through which the metal fitting can be slipped for cleaning, will prevent the polish from scratching and dulling the surrounding leather or getting into the thread holes where it dries to form a white residue. The pad terrets and

49  Miss Penny Fitzgerald driving her Dales mare, Stainton Darkie, to a modern ralli car during the marathon phase of a combined driving event

bearing-rein hook can be carefully unscrewed for cleaning then replaced, taking care not to damage the screw thread. A tiny drop of oil on the tongues of the hame tug and other larger buckles will keep them free moving. Now that steel bits which took hours of cleaning with sharp sand and paraffin concoctions are virtually things of the past, modern stainless steel bits only require a rinse in warm water to clean them, while nickel bits should have the cheeks, but not the mouthpiece, cleaned with liquid metal polish and a cloth.

## Care of driving whips

There is only one way in which to store bow-top driving whips and that is on a whipreel which is a flat, circular wooden device with a V-shaped notch running around the outer edge and into which the thong of the whip is nipped. Using a reel prevents the stock of the whip from warping as it may if propped up in a corner or laid flat, and the shepherd's crook shape at the top is maintained by the curve of the reel. Drop thong whips can be hung from hooks on the wall to again prevent the stock from warping. Occasionally the thong can be wiped over with saddle soap to keep it supple but the old practice of chalking thongs to keep them white should not be emulated.

### Making your own whip

For those people who would like to make their own whip, the most difficult part is finding a suitable stock. Although a number of different types of wood are suitable, holly that has grown on stony ground is best as it will have grown slowly and will therefore be stronger. A straight, evenly-tapering second-growth shoot of six to seven years of age should be selected, although some people prefer a dog-leg stock, which is shaped like the hind leg of a dog with two right angle bends, as they believe it balances better in the hand and prevents rainwater trickling up the driver's sleeve. The stick should be hung in a dry, well-ventilated place until thoroughly seasoned and, if a weight is tied to the end, this will help to keep the stock straight as it dries out. The bark can then be stripped off and the bare wood stained using wood dye. Attractive markings can be produced by using a light coloured stain, varnishing the stock then, when it is dry, sandpapering the knots lightly or paring very tiny flakes of wood off the full length of the stock before rubbing a rag dipped in dark coloured dye over the whole thing. The darker stain will only be able to colour the parts where the varnish has been removed. Several top coats of varnish should be applied to form a tough protective coating. A saddler will be able to fit a leather handle and a thong, although bow-top thongs with integral quills can be bought from driving accessories suppliers and fitted at home using non-water soluble glue and a binding of black thread. If preferred, a small metal butt end can be fitted in place of a leather handle although the latter gives a better grip, especially in wet weather.

## SUMMARY

**When a vehicle is being stored:**

- Keep in a dry, well ventilated building out of sunlight
- Support shafts to keep them off the ground
- Block up the axle so the wheels are clear of the ground and can rotate freely
- Grease axles thoroughly
- Cover the vehicle with a light dust sheet

**Regular maintenance of equipment:**

- Clean harness thoroughly after use and store on brackets
- Check harness regularly for wear, loose stitching or breakages
- Wash vehicles down after use and check for damage
- Keep driving whips on a whip reel
- Store carriage lamps safely where the glass panes cannot be broken
- Keep driving aprons folded in a drawer

# GLOSSARY

**AXLE ARM** – the shaped end of the axle on which the wheel of the vehicle rotates. Sometimes called the axle tree.

**AXLE BED** – the centre part of the axle to which the axle arms are attached at either end.

**AXLE BOX** – the centre of the hub of the wheel into which the axle arm is fixed.

**BUGGY** – in America a general term for four-wheeled owner-driver vehicles. In Britain the term is sometimes used to describe a hooded gig.

**BOX** – raised driving seat, especially on coachman-driven vehicles.

**BOX LOOP** – box-shaped leather keeper on harness in which the buckled point of a strap lies.

**CARRIAGE JACK** – levering device to raise and support the end of the axle while the wheel is removed to grease the axle tree.

**CHAMFER** – the shaving or planing of the spokes or framework of a vehicle to improve the appearance and reduce the weight.

**CHANNEL** – the metal rim attaching the rubber tyre to the felloes of a wheel.

**CHASSIS** – the metal or wooden undercarriage of a vehicle.

**COUPLING REIN** – the short piece of a pair rein buckled onto the longer draught rein.

**CUTTER** – a type of sleigh with elegant curved runners.

**DASHBOARD** – raised protective board in front of the driving seat.

**DICKEY** – a seat for grooms at the back of a carriage. Sometimes called a rumble.

**DISH** – type of wheel having spokes set into the hub at an angle to give a concave appearance.

**DROP** – decorative part of harness which lies on the horse's forehead. Also known as the face-piece.

**DUTCH COLLAR** – another name for a breast collar.

**EVENER** – an American term for a swingletree.

**FELLOES** – sections of the wheel rim into which the spokes are fitted.

**FENDER** – an American term for a splashboard or mudguard.

**FOOTBOARD** – raised board at the front of a driving seat to support the feet.

**FUTCHELL** – wooden or metal arm projecting from the forecarriage of a vehicle to which the shaft or splinter bar is attached.

**GERMAN SILVER** – used for harness and shaft fittings. Also known as white brass or albata.

**HEAD** – a roof or hood on a vehicle.

**HITCH** – in America a generic term for any turnout.

**INDISPENSION UNIT** – a modern form of suspension in which each wheel is individually attached to the vehicle by an angled arm culminating in a square steel spindle set into a box lined with high density rubber. Jolting from the wheels is absorbed by the spindle turning against the rubber lining.

**LEAF SPRINGS** – springs made up from flat, curved plates of tempered steel.

**NAFF** – term used in some parts of England for a wheel hub.

**NAVE** – another term for a wheel hub.

**PERCH** – the longitudinal bar between the front and rear axles of some vehicles around which the undercarriage was built.

**RIG** – American term for a complete turnout or a vehicle on its own.

**ROLLER BOLT** – attachment on a splinter bar to which the trace is attached.

**SPLINTER BAR** – crossbeam on the forecarriage of a four-wheeled vehicle to which the shafts, pole or swingletree may be fitted.

**SWINGLETREE** – horizontal bar to which the traces are attached on some types of vehicle.

**TANDEM** – two horses driven one in front of the other.

**WHIFFLETREE** – a swingletree between the shafts of a two-wheeled vehicle.

# USEFUL ADDRESSES

## Suppliers and Craft Firms

### United Kingdom

Artistic Iron Products, Sparrow Lane, Long Bennington, Newark, Notts. (Horse-drawn vehicle manufacturers)

James Asbridge (Greenwich) Ltd., 60 Banning Street, London (Coach builders and coach painters)

Bridleways of Guildford Ltd., Smithbrook Kilns, Rural Craft Centre, near Cranleigh, Surrey (Harness makers)

Ron Conibear, 5 The Square, Vicarage Farm Road, Peterborough, Cambs. (Wheelwright and vehicle repairer)

Croford Coachbuilders Ltd., Dover Place, Ashford, Kent (Carriage builders and wheelwrights)

The Crowland Carriage Company, Head Office, Dirnanean Estate, Enochdhu, Strathardle, Perthshire, Scotland (Manufacturers of new vehicles)

Jon and Christine Dick, Old Green End Farm, Kensworth, Bedfordshire (Driving tuition; horses broken and trained to harness)

Peter Durrant, 7 Cordys Lane, Trimley St. Mary, Ipswich, Suffolk (Coach painting, lining, gilding and heraldic designs)

Richard and Vivian Ellis, Coles Farm, Cleverton, Chippenham, Wiltshire (Driving tuition)

Fairbourne Carriages, The Oast House, Fairbourne Mill, Harrietsham, Kent (Carriage builder and restorer, coach painting and leatherwork; suppliers of driving accoutrements; vehicles for sale)

Fenix Carriage and Driving Centre, East Ruckham, Cruwys Morchard, near Tiverton, Devon (New horse-drawn vehicles; driving instruction)

W. & H. Gidden Ltd., 112/122 Tabernacle Street, London (Harness makers)

Richard Gill & Sons, Brame Lane, Norwood, Harrogate, North Yorkshire (Carriage builders and restorers; suppliers of parts and fittings)

A. & H. Green, 237 Forest Road, Woodhouse, Loughborough, Leics. (Show, working and exercise harness made to measure)

Gryphin Harness, Glanyrafon Estate, Aberystwyth, Dyfed, Wales (Makers of competition and exercise harness)

Alfred Hales, Manor Road, Wales, near Sheffield, Yorkshire (Carriage lamp manufacturer; supplier of all types of carriage fittings)

Matthew Harvey & Co. Ltd., Bath Street, Walsall, Staffordshire (Bit makers)

Keith Luxford (Saddlery) Ltd., 57 High Street, Teddington, Middlesex (Harness makers)

Naylors Saddlery Ltd., 472 Edenfield Road, Rochdale, Lancashire (Suppliers of show harness, holly whips, bits, gloves, aprons, lamps, etc.)

C.J. Nicholson, Sandy Close Farm, Sherfield English, Romsey, Hampshire (Carriage Builder)

Red House Stables, Old Road, Darley Dale, Matlock, Derbyshire (Driving tuition; horses broken to harness)

Ride and Drive, 66 Valley Road, Kenley, Surrey (Made to measure driving harness; also driving accessories)

Tedman Harness, 58 Clifden Road, Worminghall, Buckinghamshire (Show and exercise harness makers; also driving accoutrements)

Thimbleby & Shorland, 31 Great Knollys Street, Reading, Berkshire (Carriage, harness and driving accoutrement auctioneers)

John Thompson, 1 Fieldway, Fleet, Hampshire (Carriage building plans)

Turf & Travel Saddle and Harness Centre, 93 High Street, Eton, Berks. (Harness suppliers)

Turner-Bridgar, 21 Wallingford Road, Goring on Thames, Reading, Berks. (Harness makers)

Sallie Walrond, Thorne Lodge, Cockfield, Bury St. Edmunds, Suffolk (Driving tuition)

Wellington Carriage Company, Long Lane, Telford, Shropshire (Carriage builders and restorers)

John Willie's Saddle Room Ltd., Burley, Hampshire (Carriage builders and harness makers)

Withybrook Carriages, Featherbed Lane, Withybrook, near Coventry, Warwickshire (Carriage restoration and painting; vehicles for sale; suppliers of driving harness and accoutrements)

Charles Wylie, Waterford, 23 Kingholme Road, Dumfries, Scotland (Designer and builder of carriages)

Jackdaw Harness, Daw Bank, Greenholme, Tebay, Penrith, Cumbria (Harness makers)

## United States and Canada

American Four-in-Hand Training Centre, R.D. 2, Martin Road, Auburn, New York, USA. (Horses broken and trained; driving tuition; suppliers of horse-drawn vehicles, harness and related accessories)

Brasses Unlimited, 740 Morningside Drive, Englewood, Florida, USA. (Suppliers of harness, lamps, whips, umbrella baskets and all driving accessories)

Burkholder Buggy Shop, Dayton, Virginia, 22821, USA (New Vehicles built and supplied. Also spare parts and repairs.)

Freedman Harness Ltd., 1875 Dundas Street, West Toronto, Canada. (Harness makers)

Russell Hardwick, Hardwick Hideout, Route 6, Box 365HH, Silver Spring, Florida, USA (Manufacturer of aluminium carriages)

Hickory Ridge Carriage and Harness Shop, Earlesville, Virginia, USA (Repair, restoration and sale of harness and vehicles; driving accessories supplied; driving instruction given)

Kasica Carriage Company, 19121 Rogers Road, Odessa, Florida, USA (Dealers in old and new carriages and harness)

Lapp's Coach Shop, 3572 West Newport Road, Ronks, Pennsylvania, USA (Carriage restorers; carriage parts; vehicles for sale)

William Lower, Millington Driving Centre, Route 1, State Route 665, Box 178, Free Union, Virginia, USA (Horses broken and trained to harness)

Martin Auctioneers Inc., P.O. Box 477, Intercourse, Pennsylvania, USA (Carriage, harness and driving accoutrement auctioneers)

Montana Carriage Company, 7457 Highway 2 East, P.O. Box 158, Columbia Falls, Montana, USA (Builders of horse-drawn vehicles)

Robeson Saddlery Ltd., 3808 Rush-Mendon Road, P.O. Box 221, Mendon, New York, USA (Harness makers)

Smuckers Harness Shop, RD3, Navron (Churchtown), Pennsylvania, USA (Makers of all types of harness)

Wagon Works, 40 Bachelor Street, West Newbury, Massachusetts, USA (Vehicles built and restored; carriage lamps and accessories)

Weaverton Coach Shop, 3007, Old Philadelphia Pike, Bird in Hand, Pennsylvania, USA (Carriage restorers; vehicles for sale)

## *Driving Societies*

British Driving Society, 27 Dugard Place, Barford, Warwickshire

American Driving Society, P.O. Box 160, Metamara, M1 48455-0160, USA

Carriage Association of America, RD1, Box 115, Salem, NJ 08079

# FURTHER READING

Here are some books that may be of use and interest.

H.R.H. THE DUKE OF EDINBURGH, *Competitive Driving*, Horsedrawn Carriages Ltd (out of print)

ELLIS, V. and R., and CLAXTON, J., *Donkey Driving*, J.A. Allen, 1980

ISLES, G.L., *The Restoration of Carriages*, J.A. Allen, 1981

JOHNSON, J., *Competition Driving on a Shoestring*, J.A. Allen, 1990

KNIGHT, Capt. C. MORLEY., *Hints on Driving*, J.A. Allen. 1970

LORCH, W., *Competition Carriage Vehicles, Choice, Construction, Maintenance*, J.A. Allen, 1991

PAPE, M., *The Art of Driving*, J.A. Allen, 1982

RICHARDSON, C., *Driving, The Development and Use of Horsedrawn Vehicles*, B.T. Batsford 1985

RYDER, T., *On The Box Seat*, Horsedrawn Carriages Ltd, 1969

SMITH, D.J.M., *A Dictionary of Horsedrawn Vehicles*, J.A. Allen, 1988

WALROND, S., *A Guide to Driving Horses*, Pelham Horsemaster Series (out of print)

WALROND, S., *Breaking a Horse to Harness*, J.A. Allen, 1989

WALROND, S., *Looking at Carriages*, J.A. Allen. 1992

WALROND, S., *The Encyclopaedia of Carriage Driving*, J.A. Allen, 1988

# INDEX